Where Maple Leaves Fell

Where Maple Leaves Fell

PROFILES THE MURDER OF CANADIAN
POWS ONLY HOURS AFTER D-DAY

JOHN GILBERT

Copyright 2009 © by John Gilbert. All rights reserved. No part of this book may be reproduced or used in any form or by any means, electronic or mechanical, including photocopying, recording, or in any information storage and retrieval system, without permission in writing from the publisher.

Published by Gargunnock Books
Coppelia
14 Papercourt Lane
Ripley Woking
Surrey GU23 6DS

Cover Design by Graeme Wadhams, ably assisted by Owen Miles.

Printed and Interior Design by Kall Kwik Woking.
Special thanks to Mark Warner, Director and David Bedford.
mark@woking.kallkwik.co.uk

Includes bibliographical references.

ISBN 978-0-9561723

THE AUTHOR

John H. C Gilbert was born in 1946. He was educated at Rydens Secondary Modern School, Walton-on-Thames, Surrey, and served almost thirty years in the Surrey Police, attaining the rank of Inspector. From his home in the Surrey village of Ripley, situated only one mile from the R.H.S. Garden at Wisley, he now writes about Canada's participation in the Battle for Normandy. The son of a French Canadian tank gunner, his specialised topic is the fierce and often brutal fighting to liberate Caen, Field Marshal Montgomery's most treasured D-Day objective!

By the same Author:

Bloody Buron! Canada's D-Day + 1.
ISBN 0-9735614-1-6

Only Death Could Land. The Canadian attack on Carpiquet - July 1944.
ISBN 0-9735614-0-8

And, as welcome break from the horrors of war!

Fun, Flies & Laughter - A Stirling Life!
ISBN 0 7223 3786-8
Arthur H. Stockwell Ltd
www.ahstockwell.co.uk

TABLE OF CONTENTS

Dedication

Introduction

Chapter 1   Push for Carpiquet . . . . Page 15

Chapter 2   Ambushed 21

Chapter 3   They Only Eat Our Rations 32

Chapter 4   Déjà-vu at Carpiquet 43

Chapter 5   The Beast of Caen 57

Chapter 6   Captured and Caged 66

Chapter 7   The Trial of Kurt Meyer 73

Chapter 8   Murder in War is still Murder! 92

Postscript   99

Photo credits

Bibliography

Endnotes

Acknowledgements

DEDICATION

IN MEMORY OF BRAVE CANADIAN PRISONERS OF WAR - EXECUTED AT THE L' ANCIENNE ABBAYE D' ARDENNE IN THE PROVINCE OF NORMANDY AND THE REPUBLIC OF FRANCE ON OR ABOUT THE 7ᵀᴴ DAY OF JUNE 1944 IN VIOLATION OF THE LAWS AND USAGES OF WAR.

On the night of June 7/8, 1944, 18 Canadian soldiers were murdered in this garden while being held here as prisoners of war. Two more prisoners died here or nearby on June 17. They are dead but not forgotten.

Nestling within the sacred grounds of the ancient Abbey, sits a bronze memorial tablet honouring those eighteen Canadian prisoners of war, all of whom were cruelly executed on or about the night of June 7, 1944.

The poignant inscription reads as above:

Killed on or about June 07, 1944

THE SHERBROOKE FUSILIER REGIMENT

Lieutenant Thomas A. L. Windsor	Age 29	Montreal, PQ
Trooper Harold George Philp	Age 32	Manilla, Ont
Trooper Roger Lockhead	Age 25	Montreal, PQ
Trooper Thomas H. Henry	Age 22	Montreal, PQ
Trooper James Elgin Bolt	Age 24	St Thomas, Ont
Trooper George Vincent Gill	Age 23	England

THE NORTH NOVA SCOTIA HIGHLANDERS

Corporal Joseph F. MacIntrye	Age 28	Sydney Mines, NS
Private Ivan Lee Crowe	Age 22	New Glasgow, NS
Private Charles Doucette	Age 31	Sydney, NS
Private Hollis Leslie McKeil	Age 23	Lower Selmah, NS
Private James Alvin Moss	Age 22	Stellarton, NS
Private Walter Michael Doherty	Age 22	Galway, NB
Private Reginald Keeping	Age 21	Burgeo, Nfld
Private Hugh Allen MacDonald	Age 24	Morvan, NS
Private George Edward Millar	Age 19	Pembroke, Ont
Private Thomas Edward Mont	Age 23	Truro, NS
Private Raymond Moore	Age 27	Kentville, NS
Private George R. McNaughton	Age 20	Sydney, NS

Killed on June 17, 1944

THE STORMONT, DUNDAS AND GLENGARRY HIGHLANDERS

Lieutenant Frederick Williams	Age 22	Dalton, England
Lance Corporal George G. Pollard	Age 19	Cornwall, Ont

INTRODUCTION

"He knew the essence of war is violence and moderation in war is imbecility"
Lord Thomas B. Macaulay 1800-1859

There are two fundamental reasons for re-examining the acts of unhinged cruelty that led to the callous deaths of eighteen Canadian soldiers; all heartlessly and simultaneously executed within the sacred grounds of the L' Ancienne Abbaye d' Ardenne. To pay a lasting and fitting tribute - each having died as a prisoner of war in the best traditions of the service simply because they refused to betray their comrades or their country by giving information to the enemy. And, to determine whether or not the ruthless Nazi commander SS-Standartenführer (Colonel) Kurt "Panzer" Meyer was either agreeable or apathetic towards the pitiless killings and as a consequence guilty of war crimes! (Having immediately recognised that the lofty towers of the ancient structure afforded the very best views of the impending battlefield, the astute Meyer had cunningly tailored the former and rather imposing sanctuary into a forward command post).

With a great deal of irony, the cruel deaths of these fresh-faced Canadian volunteers led by the enthusiastic career soldier Major-General R.F.L. Kellor, sprang from the outstanding triumphs of Operation Overlord, known universally as D-Day! In particular the impressive Canadian push inland during June 7, 1944, the following day. (Incidentally the prefix "D-" relates to the opening of any critical action, although Supreme Allied Commander, General Eisenhower always used the term "D-Dog Day.") Subsequently, the dramatic events described in this following short synopsis, would inevitably go down in the annals of military history.

> "H-Hour, the time designated for the British and
> Canadian troops to hit the beach ranged between
> 0725 and 0745. We would be above them"
> Flying Officer R. Rohmer. [1]

After several days of boredom and of cursing the poor, wet English weather, followed by hours of being crammed within landing craft awash in a cocktail of salt water, oil, vomit and urine; units of the 3rd Canadian Division (the 7th and 8th Canadian Infantry Brigades) quickly and bravely fought for the French shore. After arriving on schedule, they had pursued the intense naval shelling (from the cruisers H.M.S. Belfast and H.M.S. Diadem) that had stunned an amazed enemy. Their resolve in eliminating almost all-enemy resistance and securing their designated area of beach (code-named Juno) subsequently enabled the Reserve 9th (Highland) Brigade to disembark comparatively safely and then thrust inland towards Caen. By nightfall, leading elements of the brigade had formed a fortress based on the high ground around the cross-roads near the village Villons les Buissons, situated only a few miles north of the historic and significant city. And, while less optimistic commanders could claim that the Canadians role in the Overlord objective had not been entirely successful, Eisenhower and the whole of the allied senior command were jubilant!

As soon as dawn broke, matters became surprisingly more complex and as the day progressed, far more demanding. As expected, the Canadians were immediately ordered to link up with the British Reserve 9th Brigade and then continue with General Montgomery's original D-Day plan: to seize Caen! Indeed, these two highly respected attack brigades - coincidently both reserve brigades - were expected to cut a dash in military history not only by capturing the city but also the strategically important airfield at Carpiquet to the west.

Alone, and unaware of mounting difficulties the Canadians boldly pushed towards Carpiquet. Regrettably, just as the airfield objective became clearly in view, the brigade's armoured strike force -

the Sherbrooke Fusiliers and the infantrymen of North Nova Scotia Highlanders - were suddenly ambushed by a sudden colossus of steel hurled at them by the fanatical Nazi and war criminal.

Unfortunately for the Canadians, their opponents on that fateful day were the elite, political "boy" soldiers of the Hitler Youth, the 12th SS Panzer Division. Soon to earn the reputation as the "Murder Division," Meyer's regiment and several other units of the Hitlerjugend had cunningly taken advantage of the Canadians' exposed and highly vulnerable left flank. Regrettably, a series of unexpected difficulties had earlier befallen the equally unlucky British 9th Brigade, which meant that despite several determined efforts, the intended link up with the Canadians failed to materialise. And as a direct result, Meyer had been able to organize a surprise attack, just in the nick of time.

Another unpleasant shock for the Canadian 9th Brigade was that this elite adversary, comprised of experienced officers and extremely ruthless NCOs, was lavishly equipped with superior tanks and weapons, particularly the merciless 88-mm anti-tank gun and the cruel and deadly killing power of a mortar battalion equipped with the lethal Nebelwefer. The safe arrival of this potent force enabled enemy grenadiers to effectively rain down salvoes of rocket-style mortar shells into the leading formations of Shermans and exposed infantry. Sadly, statistics reveal that in the hands of the Meyer's grenadiers, these formidable weapons were to continue to cause devastating casualties during Canadian operations. (Highly relevant, was that prior to being formerly established on June 24, 1943, to ensure that the Hitlerjugend would be imbued with the essential fighting qualities of an elite division, cadre personnel had been transferred from Hitler's bodyguard division (literally Lifeguard Regiment of Adolf Hitler-LAH) the formidable Leibstandarte-SS Adolf Hitler. This decision did not only underscore the two divisions intimate ties but also created a feared and effective killing machine!)

As light began to fade on that grim June 8, there was yet another cruel twist of fate. For eighteen Canadian prisoners, the cessation of combat did not signify an end to their ordeal: Meyer's grenadiers executed them. What's more, these pitiless killings were committed; while he, their commander, was present and only footsteps away.

To help develop a deeper appreciation of how this ungodly act of barbarism adversely affected Canadian morale, the atrocities at the abbey together with other murders are covered in some depth. The narrative then unfolds by revealing how gathering rumours (and quickly thereafter the bitter news that confirmed the killings) gave many incensed Canucks an insight as to how war against the SS, should from then on be conducted. For many, their understanding of what was now required was perfectly clear. In future, they too would wage war without displaying mercy to the enemy.

Consequently, these dire circumstances also inspire a need to study the provocative career and audacious leadership of SS-Brigadeführer Meyer. (On June 14, Meyer was promoted to Divisional Commander) For those historians that have failed to recognize the Brigadeführer's impact on the struggle for Caen, this closer inspection will prove enlightening. The study clearly reveals two highly significant factors: Meyer's daring, and his utter ruthlessness. These attributes are especially noticeable during the cruel fighting around Buron and Authie, and during the merciless conflict at the nearby village of Carpiquet a month later!

As a result, the question also arises as to Meyer's culpability for his troops' callous actions in and around the abbey grounds where most of the Canadian prisoners met their deaths. Whereas an in depth study of his trial is particularly crucial, it is also essential to re-examine the extent of equally appalling Canadian reprisals during the fighting around Carpiquet and its airfield. And thereafter consider how these factors may have adversely affected those who sat in judgement in Meyer's war crimes hearing, principally in the final sentencing.

In seeking the truth, however, other critical issues must be understood. First, the philosophy of this book should be made perfectly clear: whatever else this re-investigation may be, it is intended neither to criticize nor overlook the gallantry displayed by those Canadian and German soldiers who fought so savagely against one another. Secondly, there is a moral principle to be considered. However misguided those young Germans may have been, it was acutely obvious that they and the Canadians each firmly believed that their own particular cause was completely justified, thus making any comment that denounces their efforts an unwise indictment against their deeply felt sense of patriotism. And while the sensitivity surrounding this topic is fully appreciated and the hindsight common to so many armchair critics is to be avoided, there still remains a need to unravel those few remaining anomalies.

Significantly however, Where Maples Leaves Fell is not in any way an official account of Kurt Meyer's war crimes trial, nor is it intended as more than partial history of the Canadians courageous role in the battle for Normandy. It is simply an honest amalgam of factual official war diaries, authentic archive records and reports, added to a personal re-examination of both the atrocities, and Meyer's highly questionable culpability. (Of the 1017 fatalities suffered by 3rd Canadian Infantry Division and 2nd Canadian Armoured Brigade - 1 in 7 were at the hands of their captors!) Its other main focus is to pay fitting tribute to all those brave Canadian volunteers who took part in the campaign to liberate North-West Europe from Nazi oppression; particularly those either wounded or killed. (By August 31, Canadian military casualties stood at 1,324 officers and 18,623 other ranks; of these, 340 officers 4,285 other ranks had been killed or had died) With a special tribute to those heroic Maple Leaf Canadians so callously executed within the sacred grounds of the L' Ancienne Abbaye d' Ardenne.

One

PUSH FOR CARPIQUET

"The 9th Brigade moved on towards Carpiquet – the vanguard group consisted of the North Nova Scotia Highlanders supported by the whole of the 27th Armoured Regiment"
- Colonel C.P. Stacey, O.B.E. Director,
Historical Section, General Staff

In the early hours of June 7, 1944, the volunteers of the Canadian 3rd Division's (reserve, now spearhead) 9th Brigade, most of whom had experienced a relatively uneventful D-Day landing, began to anxiously prepare for the day ahead. For the brigade's armoured strike force—the Sherbrooke Fusiliers (27th Armoured Regiment) and the infantrymen of the North Nova Scotia Highlanders (NNSH)—the logistics involved in an armoured column and an infantry regiment waking, stirring, and getting ready for action on that morning would have been almost identical to the routine on so many other days of wearisome early-morning starts. Yet events that had interrupted that short night had left everyone acutely aware that this day was going to be somewhat different from any other.

At around 0200 hours, enemy infantry, who were particularly well armed and somewhat surprisingly equipped with half-track vehicles, had suddenly attacked positions held by both the Highlanders and the French-Canadians of the Régiment de la

Chaudière. Although this opening skirmish had been dealt with quickly and successfully, the daring German enterprise had been another cruel reminder to the loyal Canadians that the day ahead was not going to be another of familiar and seemingly endless war games. In addition to a few regrettable casualties, another specific cause for real concern was the calibre of the enemy. These night time raiders were not run-of-mill troops from the nearby static (coastal) 716th Division under the command of Generalleutnant Wilhelm Richter; they were instead reconnaissance grenadiers from the advancing 21st Panzer Division, a reconstruction of Rommel's old Africa Corps! (192nd Panzer Grenadier Battalion was another possible belligerent.) Perhaps even more worrying was the formidable mobility and firepower that came by way of the immensely versatile and sturdy trademark of German panzer formations, the Sdkfz 251/1 armoured personnel carrier. (These fast and well-armoured half-tracks were able to carry a crew of twelve and were fitted with two 7.92-mm machine guns.)

As night gave way to a bright warm dawn and news of the attack rapidly spread down the line, those Canadian units spared from losses could have been forgiven for feeling rather euphoric; once again they had tasted victory. The facts, however were somewhat less encouraging. In spite of facing overwhelming odds, these panzer grenadiers had caused the Régiment de la Chaudière to suffer the loss of a whole platoon (approximately 30 men, usually led by a 2nd Lieutenant).[1]

In the occupied villages to the south, within the parish of the Abbey d'Ardenne, German forces were also stirring and preparing for the day ahead. Although they too had shared a restless night, there was one major difference in their mindset. Unlike the Canadian 9th Brigade, the troops of the bedraggled German infantry, which had taken the brunt of the fighting the previous day, were well aware of what was to come. This was not their only advantage, for now they also had the comforting thought that "Panzer" Meyer was with them. Several of the unit commanders were also probably aware of the outstanding credentials of SS-Standartenführer Meyer, and of his visit during the night to discuss battle tactics.

When dawn finally arrived and while German infantry were feverishly getting their defensive plans in order, the Canadians, only a few kilometres north, rather tentatively descended from the high ground at La Mare. After having quickly regrouped and no longer in the relative safety normal for a reserve regiment, the fully laden Shermans of the Sherbrooke Fusiliers (together with their support infantry, the North Nova Scotia Highlanders) began to prepare for the short journey towards Villons Les Buissons. With this achieved and final arrangements completed, the tanks commanded by Lieutenant Colonel M. B. K. Gordon (CO of the Sherbrooke Fusiliers) started to move slowly and cautiously towards with their airfield objective in the same battle order as they had so successfully advanced during the previous D-Day evening. The light yet faster Stuart tanks of the reconnaissance troop led. Behind them, riding on the battalion's carriers, came "C" Company of the North Nova Scotia Highlanders. Next came a platoon of medium machine guns from the Cameron Highlanders of Ottawa, a troop of tank destroyers (17-pounders) of the divisional anti-tank regiment, two sections of pioneers, and four battalion 6-pounders. Behind this vanguard came the main body of the advance guard: three infantry companies of the North Nova Scotia Highlanders riding on the Sherbrookes' armour.

At first, German opposition was slight but quickly became more troublesome as the vanguard approached the village of Buron. With the knowledge of having an SS Panzer Division at their side, a far more confident enemy was carrying out the hastily devised plan to hinder and frustrate the Canadian advance by implementing spoiling tactics until midday, when the Hitlerjugend and the 21st Panzer Division would coordinate and then mount their planned twin counterattack. The day was still young, and the German armour was not yet ready to go on the offensive. The decisive battle was still more than four long hours away.

The notion that the village of Buron was occupied and secured by the Canadians by 1150 hours was founded on ill-based optimism; the ensuing few hours would witness several rapid changes in the occupancy of the village. In keeping with his overall account of that day's action, the Official Canadian Historian C. P. Stacey pays little attention to the struggle to liberate Buron and as a result fails to give due justice to the true intensity of the encounter. In absolute contrast, however, Canadian war diaries and several action reports speak of fierce resistance by German troops invigorated by the assumed presence of more combat-hardened grenadiers from the 21st Panzer formations. Somewhat surprisingly, reports of dogged resistance are also refuted by the chief operations officer of the 12th SS Panzer Division, Sturmbannführer Hubert Meyer (no relation to Kurt Meyer), who describes the resistance at the village as being weak and makes no mention of the involvement of grenadiers of the 21st Panzer Division. "Buron was captured by the Canadians after the weak resistance by stragglers from the 716th Infantry Division. It had been overcome at approximately 11.50 hours."[2] Although this abrupt, scornful statement fails to recognize the presence of panzer grenadiers at Buron, it provides an excellent example of the arrogance that Hubert and Kurt Meyer had in common. However, despite the unfavourable opinions that both men shared of other German units in the locality, Hubert Meyer does acknowledge the earlier action by panzer grenadiers around the vicinity of Villons-les-Buissons. The Sturmbannführer also confirms the loss of several armoured personnel carriers (Sdkfz 251/1: half-tracks).[3]

Interestingly enough, the post-combat report written by a Sherbrooke tank commander, (Sergeant T. C. Reid "C" Squadron) helps to clarify matters. His versions of events in and around Buron that morning makes the aloof comments of Sturmbannführer Meyer appear particularly churlish. "We go and for one hour we are in the centre of the heaviest mortar fire I could ever imagine and I was glad to once more hear my troop leader order us back to a small orchard, where he quickly outlined our next job which was to assist 'C' Company, I believe the NNSH, to clean out the towns code named Rhine and Danube. I believe their proper names were Authie and Buron, however just as we were set to go Mr Maclean severely damaged his right wrist caused by catching it with the counter balance of his gun. It was badly swollen and painful looking, I believe it was broken so he put me in point tank position. (Point position would lead the troop.) We blasted all the houses, holding up our infantry in the first town (Buron) and put two machine gun positions out. Then on to the next town. I no sooner got going than they opened up with small arms fire, we answered with our co-ax and they shut up. Mr Maclean and Cpl. Quinn were deployed to my left and knocking off fleeing infantry who kept on popping up in front and instead of surrendering, just either shot it out or ran."[4]

This firsthand account hardly sounds like a description of a second-rate enemy short of courage and determination. More to the point, Sergeant Reid's quite amazing action report makes utterly absurd any attempt to abruptly classify these ferocious—almost kamikaze-like—counterattacks as weak. While Reid's contrasting account may well appear reasonable, in strict military terms it may also be perfectly acceptable for more senior officers, well back in the relative safety of the rear echelons, to apply a much broader overview of the term resistance. All in all, however, to those with at least some knowledge of the encounter Sturmbannführer Meyer's dismissive summing up must surely appear discourteous and utterly mystifying.

Despite unquestionable bravery and all the various frustrations caused by resolute German spoiling tactics (particularly the very heavy mortar and rocket fire), the resolute Canadian advance towards Carpiquet was progressing far too quickly. This had resulted in the foremost tanks and the leading infantry units unwisely advancing beyond the covering range of their own protective artillery. As soon as the perilous situation was fully recognized, Lieutenant-Colonel Charles Petch, commanding the Canadian infantry and worried about compromising his success, acted as any astute leader would have done in the circumstances: he withdrew his leading troops from Authie to form a battalion strong point on the rising ground north of the village.[5] Thereafter, knowing that the majority of his support infantry were now far less compromised, Lieutenant Colonel Gordon ordered his twin attack squadrons ("A" & "B") and several Sherman's of the reserve "C" Squadron to push towards Carpiquet and its adjacent airfield.

For a short while the highly focused advance went exceeding well, a truly daring experience that was also recorded by the resourceful Sergeant Reid. "Mr MacLean came up on his 'B' set (inter-squadron radio) and told me to halt and take out an enemy hornet (German panzer) which I couldn't see; but pulling up a little further I discovered two of them at about a distance of 8 or 9 hundred yards. He instructed me to take the one left and my gunner Tpr Gilbert LJ lifted the copula into the air with his first, his 2nd and 3rd shots burnt said tank up. In the meanwhile either Sergeant Cathcart who had come and joined us or Lt MacLean, I couldn't truthfully say, blew the other hornet up. We then on and I saw that B Sqn had joined us. We were running line abreast. And although I hadn't noticed, Lieut. E. S. Spafford had pulled into the show on our right. The first house we came to (possibly Franqueville), gave forth machine gun fire so I lobbed H. E. (high explosive) in the windows. Those who ran out to the road got smacked down by Mr Spafford's guns and those who ran to the left were caught by Sgt. Cathcart, Mr Maclean and Cpl. Quinn. We shoved on again and it was a breeze. Nothing but infantry until we were fired on by an A/T gun to our right.[6]

Two

AMBUSHED

"Within minutes, most of our tanks had been knocked out, everything happened so fast, we never had a chance. The Shermans went up like torches, explosions first, fire, smoke and screaming men."
- Sgt. Dudka, North Nova Scotia Highlanders

All the while the Canadian 9th Brigade had been engaged in their struggle to clear Buron and Authie, Kurt Meyer had been watching, eagerly waiting for his chance to take up the challenge and tackle the enemy head on. The confident Meyer was no doubt champing at the bit to show the Canadian commanders that, regardless of their initial success, as they pushed towards the west of Caen and its airfield at Carpiquet, he remained in complete control of the situation and of their immediate destiny. Earlier that morning around 1000 hours, just on the outskirts of City, he had witnessed the welcome arrival of some of his divisional tanks (Panzer IVs and Panthers) and grenadiers of his own regiment; the 25th Panzergrenadiers. A short time before, after having supervised the setting up of his main Regimental Headquarters at St. Germain just west of Caen, he had driven towards the front, whereupon without any hesitation he had selected the imposing Abbaye d'Ardenne as his forward command and observation post. A high and particularly

Abbaye d'Ardenne.

sturdy stonewall surrounded the abbey and inside the abbey compound were several very useful buildings that could be quickly utilised as troop quarters and various stores. Of more importance was that the twin towers situated on both flanks of the old abbey afforded Meyer the very best views of the battlefield, and through binoculars he could see as far as the coast. After surveying and marvelling at the huge coastal buildup of troops, equipment and more importantly artillery pieces and tanks, he somehow managed to clear some very angry thoughts from his mind concerning the ineffectiveness of the once dominant Luftwaffe. His professionalism shone through; recriminations were for later; right then it was time to focus his full attention upon the advancing Canadians. From his newly acquired magnificent vantage point he could immediately identify infantry and armour moving through and around Buron and its southerly neighbour Authie. What's more, he also witnessed that Canadian determination was successfully brushing aside whatever resistance Generalleutnant Richter could muster. With an uncanny eye for detail, he quickly realized the full significance of dogged Canadian progress. "If they were not stopped at once, the Canadians would sweep through the airfield at Carpiquet, cut the two main roads west of Caen, and disrupt the whole German plan of reinforcement."[1] Once again Meyer must have felt a fusion of excitement, anger, and betrayal. By then his forward reconnaissance patrols would have told him that the Luftwaffe flak troops tasked to defend Carpiquet and its airfield had abandoned their formidable defences. (There are claims that their hasty decision came immediately after they heard rumours of successful Allied landings.) This upsetting news was just another unsavoury indignity not to be lost on Meyer, who by then must have witnessed courageous infantry troops, much maligned by others and at times by Meyer himself, giving up their lives in the forlorn hope of steadying the Canadian advance. Unquestionably, he would have contrasted their gallant actions with those of the missing Luftwaffe personnel.

After Meyer had cleared his head of anger and frustration and had spotted several Sherbrooke tanks at the approach roads to the airfield at Franqueville, his astute military mind turned to the task at hand. His recorded innermost thoughts are most compelling and describe in vivid detail the extremely precarious position of the advancing Canadians, who were totally oblivious to the lurking German presence and had no inkling of their impending fate: "The tanks were moving right across the front of the second battalion SS-Pz Regt 25. The enemy formation was showing us its unprotected flank. I issue orders to all battalions the artillery and tanks: Do not fire! Fire on my command only. The commander of the SS-Pz Regt 12 had positioned his command vehicle in the garden of the monastery. Wire was quickly laid to his tank and the enemy situation relayed from the tower to all the tanks. One company was in the monastery grounds and another on the reverse slop [sic] south of Franqueville, the enemy commander only seemed concerned with the airfield; it was in front of him. He already controlled it with his weapons. He did not realize that destruction awaited him on the reverse slope. As soon as his tanks crossed the Caen-Bayeax road he would run into the waiting Panzer regiment. Only a few hundred metres separated the iron monsters."[2]

Until now, Meyer had been operating directly under divisional command, which was running behind its original schedule. Aware that the I/12th SS Panzer Regiment could not move forward because of the lack of fuel and that the 26th SS Panzer Regiment was still east of the Orne, he took the initiative without any hint of uncertainty. In military terms, leadership so frequently requires a confident and flexible agenda, a sound and positive sense of timing, and the willingness to grasp the nettle. The experienced Meyer decided in an instant that as soon as the leading tanks passed Franqueville his regiment would attack, along with his armour positioned on the reverse slope. As soon as his lead battalion had reached Authie, the other battalions would then join the fight.

Having briefed the commander of the 21st Panzer Division and having requested support, Meyer began to feel the tension that inevitably came with the almost unbearable pressure that rested upon every word from his command. As his battle plans began to unfold, he rather nervously and quite suddenly gave the signal to attack: "Achtung! Panzer Marsch!"[3] Soon he would witness his boy soldiers fight. Soon those youngsters, still given rations of sweets instead of cigarettes, would earn the right to smoke together with their colleagues, most of whom had only just turned eighteen.

In just a few seconds, all around them the Canadians could hear the whining and screaming of anti-tank shells and see their devastating results. The noise suddenly diminished and eased back into the somewhat calm, monotonous drones of their Shermans. For several unfortunate fusiliers, these would be the last sounds they were to hear in their cruelly brief lives. Sergeant Dudka of the North Nova Scotia Highlanders recalls the sudden and bloody mayhem: "Within minutes, most of our tanks had been knocked out, everything happened so fast, we never had a chance. The Shermans went up like torches, explosions first, fire, smoke and screaming men!"[4]

Meyer's astute military mind had made the most of his own intelligence gathering. Total surprise and excellent leadership had contributed to this initial victory. Furthermore, placing his panzers hulls down (only their turrets showing) on the high ground had enabled his equal strength of armour to become an overwhelming force. It is surprising that any Canadian tanks survived; the Sherbrookes' forward "A" and "B" attack squadrons and several supporting Shermans of Sergeant Reid's "C" (reserve) squadron had been decimated by a sudden, pre-emptive, and deadly attack.

Alarmingly, this coordinated ambush had unfortunately exposed the Highlanders of "C" Company to an equally deadly onslaught, first by mortars and then by a sudden aggressive charge from Meyer's grenadiers. The brave infantrymen without any artillery backup and with their armoured support engulfed in a conflagration of fuel and flesh, suffered appalling losses.

Meanwhile, Lieutenant-Colonel Gordon and his headquarters squadron although thankfully spared from being under any direct attack, were utterly stunned by the distressing radio reports streaming from their forward squadron commanders. Notwithstanding the suddenness and ferocity of the assault, which would have caused a lesser man to panic, the astute Mel Gordon quickly put to one side any knee-jerk reaction to the desperate pleas for help that were probably echoing from his forward command radio set, and calmly made two significant tactical decisions. Although he obviously knew that neither critical action would be able to dramatically snatch victory from the rapidly closing jaws of defeat, he hoped that both decisions would increase the chance of an eventual stalemate. What's more, he was only too painfully aware that in this crisis, although an impasse was still possible, anything more would require a miracle. Refusing to give up without making a stand, he contacted and then directed the few remaining tanks of "C" Squadron, commanded and led by Major V. O. Walsh, to advance. (As a direct result of his gallantry and determination, Major Walsh was subsequently awarded the DSO.) They were to attack and repel a stream of enemy panzers that had capitalized on their earlier ambush. Meyer's tanks were now advancing towards the vanguard and headquarters of the regiment, and the entire situation was rapidly becoming more perilous by the minute. Lieutenant-Colonel Gordon also urged Brigade HQ to supply covering fire by whatever means possible despite the inherent dangers this course of action might incur.

The commander's first tactical directive worked splendidly; assured of further plunder, as the panzers approached they had possibly forgotten the British and Canadian strategy of holding back a reserve deployment. Suddenly, in uncommon confusion the zealous panzers decided to hold on to and consolidate their hard-won gains. In all probability, German enthusiasm for taking up the offensive had been subdued by the erroneous notion that the advancing Canadians were attacking with yet another endless column of Shermans. Since the Allies appeared to have an infinite supply of pristine battle tanks, the Germans' mistake was neither unreasonable nor surprising. Furthermore, any possible intervention by a few marauding Panzer IVs from the 21st Panzer Division had not materialized; their forces had unashamedly withdrawn to apparent safety only a few miles away.

Despite this annoying setback and the severity of the Allied naval fire (which was at last responding to Mel Gordon's earlier, unsuccessful plea for cover, and had began to rain down huge high explosive shells upon the stricken advance), Meyer's plan of attack was working well. Soon the few remaining civilians of this godforsaken little French village would witness further brutality. Having dashed through the lush, high cornfields and retaken Buron, youthful grenadiers of his 3rd battalion, all flushed with success unexpectedly fixed bayonets! They then charged out of the terror-stricken village screaming venom at "D" Company of the North Nova Scotia Highlanders, which had earlier dug in on the approach roads to Les Buissons. In the cold light of day, the thought of these youngsters undertaking their baptism under fire, actually agreeing to fix bayonets and then run like fury at entrenched defenders seems utterly amazing, and one can only guess at what their true motive might have been. Was it a crazed thirst for more bloodshed or an attempt to reap revenge for the deaths of their

Meyer's 'Zoot-suit' Hitlerjugend. (IWM)

fallen comrades? Alternatively, did Meyer's inspiring leadership and his powerfully persuasive sway over his young troops lead them to really believe that they alone could gather the kleine fische (or little fishes: the Canadians) and throw them back into the sea?

Whatever the true reason, as the sky over Buron darkened prematurely with huge plumes of oily black smoke belching from scores of burning and smouldering wrecked tanks and various other support vehicles, Meyer, tenacious as ever demanded more! Totally in control of the battle and brimming with confidence, he ordered his first battalion of the 25th SS Panzer Regiment into the fray. On this occasion, however, there was a fresh and equally unexpecting enemy: the British.

Although Meyer was very confident, his next objective was nevertheless extremely ambitious. His first battalion was to coordinate an advance together with several of its own divisional tanks from the 8th Panzer Company and assisted by addition Panzer IVs from the 21st Panzer Division. With this accomplished, they would push forward as far as Anguerny, more than five miles to the north. Although Meyer's courageous grenadiers quickly advanced as far as the southern fringes of Cambes, they were suddenly counterattacked by British tanks from the East Riding Yeomanry, an armoured regiment of the 3rd British Infantry Division that had finally managed to close an elusive gap between themselves and their Canadian allies.

Meyer, who was keen to know how this latest attack was progressing, began a tour of the freshly re-occupied ground. (Unlike most other commanders, Meyer routinely visited forward positions in the height of battle.) Almost immediately, he became totally dispirited with the situation at hand, and as the tour progressed so did his outright rage. For some unknown reason, the 21st Panzer Division had failed to join in the attack, thus allowing the enemy to gradually gather strength and consolidate. Meyer's fury and utter frustration were completely justified. His small panzer group was never intended to attack without the assistance of units from the 21st Panzer Division, which were still within striking distance of the enemy group's right flank.

Again, with speed and drive being of the utmost importance, Meyer put aside these feelings of anger and mistrust. Like his feelings of scorn for the Luftwaffe, any internal conflict or recriminations that had arisen out of his contempt for the unimpressive 21st Panzer Division could wait. Above all, what really mattered was that the alarming growth of the British advance needed to be quashed. Such was the ensuing mayhem that at one point Meyer himself had to actively encourage his young grenadiers to stop falling back and continue with the attack. "Recognizing their commander, the youths returned at once to their posts. Having steadied the faint of heart, Meyer returned to the Abbey." 5

> **I promise in the Hitler Youth**
> **To do my duty at all times**
> **In love and faithfulness**
> **To help the Führer**
> **So help me God.**

With memories of their enrolment and their Hitler Youth oath of allegiance to their master, Adolf Hitler, these grenadiers continued to harass the British and were to cause numerous casualties. Their tenacious offensive, however, was without adequate panzer support and was further weakened by the unwelcome appearance of a few Allied aircraft and continuing cover fire from the remorseless naval guns. After recognizing these difficulties, the battalion reluctantly withdrew to the southern edge of Cambes. "The withdrawal was not contested by the enemy, and the companies of the first battalion entrenched directly below the village."[6] A much later debriefing, revealed that Generalleutnant Edgar Feuchtinger, the commander of the 21st Panzer Division, had stated that he believed he had insufficient forces available for a joint attack.[7]

At the end of the day, Meyer's courageous but highly ambitious attempt to repel both the advancing Canadians and the delayed British had been thwarted by relentless and very effective naval shelling. To say the least, the awesome destructive power of these huge naval rounds must have been terrifying for friend and foe alike, let alone those poor wretched villagers entrapped in hurriedly prepared makeshift shelters. Such was the intensity of the ruthless bombardment that somewhat understandably a bloody stalemate had enveloped particularly in and around the pitiful village of Buron. And, despite of the Canadians achieving what would be known as the moral high ground, in strict military terms neither side could justify claiming victory!

A little earlier, as daylight was gently fading, under the shadows of the ancient monastery were now gathered more than a hundred and fifty Canadian prisoners, many of whom were seriously wounded. A jubilant Meyer, refusing to be disappointed by the lack of support from Generalleutnant Feuchtinger or by the extent of his own casualties, recollects how these wounded Canadians were being cared for as they lay alongside his own grenadiers: "In the monastery orchard our wounded comrades were being cared for; the young soldiers lying side by side and cheered each other up. Canadians were next to German soldiers. The doctors and medics didn't look at the uniforms. There was nothing to separate them at this point. The only thing that mattered was saving lives."[8]

Whether or not Meyer's empathetic statement affords a genuine insight into his true state of mind will be discussed in some depth later. Meanwhile, while making their way back to the abbey, the focus of several young grenadiers mainly from his 3rd battalion still high on adrenalin and with their blood on the boil, was far less compassionate. More than this, incidents of sordid reprisals, for probably having witnessed the death of comrades, provides a taste of how they would now wage war. Led by Oberstrumführer Karl-Heinz Milus, a bold, supremely confident but rather aloof fervent Nazi, these young headstrong grenadiers required calmer and far more composed leadership. Indeed, various accounts of their hysterical behaviour are particularly barbed. Having undergone their baptism of fire, more than just a few acted quite inexcusably, showing little restraint whatsoever. And, although ardent critics of Meyer could argue that their behaviour was a cogent reason behind Milus's promotion, logic tends to dispel this rationale. In fact, it was probably another example of being at the right place at the right time.

There is however little doubt that having tasted the bittersweet pill of combat, several fanatical grenadiers and a few wilful tank commanders behaved appallingly. Without any apparent reason at least six Canadians were dragged from a line of prisoners being escorted towards the abbey and taken to a nearby farmhouse. Once inside the kitchen, a pistol shot to the back of the head systematically butchered them. About the same time, "villager Louis Alaperrine was attempting to put a bandage on a Canadian, wounded by a shell, when an SS officer stepped up and shot the injured soldier twice in the head. In a separate episode, a Sherbrooke Fusilier medic wearing a Red Cross armband was gunned down while treating a wounded North Nova."[9] Equally contemptible were incidents of callous Panzer drivers deliberately tracking over wounded Canadians lying at the side of the road waiting for transport. And even more chilling, was that these acts of barbarism, was just the beginning!

Three

THEY ONLY EAT OUR RATIONS

*"He found the bodies of the Canadian soldiers
lying together in a pool of blood"*
- Lt-Col. B.J.S. MacDonald O.B.E.Q.C.

Only a few kilometres north west of the Abbey and shocked by the ordeal, the exhausted and battle-scarred Canadian 9th Brigade were beginning to improve upon their precarious positions by digging in and mounting perimeter guards. While reconnaissance patrols – desperately trying to get a fix on enemy locations – were probing into the fading light and sudden darkness, the atmosphere was probably a fusion of electric excitement and passive tension. Those lucky enough to be spared duties were inevitably reliving the experiences of their own unique action and possibly the brutal moment that ended the lives of their colleagues. All were probably wondering what was happening to those who were missing, particularly the wounded. No one among the Canadian ranks would have known or perhaps even contemplated that within a few torturous hours eighteen Canadian prisoners of war were to suffer the ultimate act of cruelty: execution! Their only possible crime was that some among them might have inflicted casualties upon their enemy. Even this understandable act of war was in their particular case most unlikely. These unfortunate men had been overwhelmed by Meyer's pre-emptive strike and were lucky just to have remained unscathed by the vicious ambush, let alone to have had the time or opportunity to actually retaliate.

It was during the morning of the following day (June 8), while the Canadian 7th Brigade was busily engaged with the Hitlerjugend's 26th SS Panzer Regiment, that a young 12th SS Panzer Kradmelder (motorcycle messenger) of Polish extraction in the division's reconnaissance unit was to witness brutality beyond belief. After having arrived at the abbey, SS-Sturmann (Lance Corporal) Jan Jesionek heard Meyer shout out angrily to a perplexed POW guard, "Why do you bring prisoners to the rear? They only eat up our rations - in future no more prisoners are to be taken."[1] Sensing trouble stirring and not wishing to get involved, Jesionek decided to scamper from the scene in order to escape any additional duties. While seemingly very able, at just seventeen, he probably did what most youngsters would have done in his situation: get away as quickly as possible from senior officers and NCOs and try to get something to eat and drink after finding an out-of-the-way place to wash and rest.

Although they were full-fledged members of the Hitlerjugend, it is worth examining the dilemma of many young German-speaking Silesian Poles. Particularly those who were involuntary inducted, yet appeared more than willing to wear the Wehrmacht grey after hearing news of Soviet atrocities. These politically confused teenagers, despite their dubious standing and willingness to fight for the Greater Reich, were still vehemently independent. Regardless of any political persuasion, their loyalty to their particular unit, no matter how esteemed its reputation, usually came a close second to their solidarity with their fellow Poles.

It was while Jesionek was washing at a pump near the abbey gardens that he saw an officer interrogating seven Canadian prisoners. "One of the prisoners had tears in his eyes, and the officer laughed at him in a sneering manner. The officer seemed to be enjoying himself and frequently burst out laughing as he spoke to the prisoners. He took their papers from them and returned to the Chapel"[2]. A few moments later he heard each of the seven prisoners being called by name and in turn directed up some steps into a nearby garden. All seemed to know what was about to happen to them; each in turn calmly shook hands with the others before leaving. Seconds after, the sound of gunshots and the occasional scream could be heard clearly. An SS-Oberschafüher, (Sergeant), who had previously positioned himself in the garden, had shot each one in the back of the head. Thereafter, Jesionek noticed the Oberschafüher emerge from the garden while reloading his pistol. Then, after having sensibly waited awhile, the young Pole entered the garden to confirm what he thought had happened. He found the dead bodies of the Canadian soldiers lying together in a large pool of blood.[3]

Those twenty-four hours included yet another crime charged against Meyer's regiment. The futile and totally unnecessary incident that subsequently took the life of Captain W. L. Brown, the Protestant chaplain attached to the Sherbrooke Fusiliers, was quite understandably the cause of intense and animated media attention both in Normandy and back in Canada.

During the night of June 7, Captain Brown, Lieutenant W. F. Granger, and Lance-Corporal J. H. Greenwood, all presumably still suffering from the shock waves of Buron, were in a jeep (driven by the padre) somewhere in the area of Galmanche, which was still occupied by Meyer's 1st Battalion. Having earlier received news of a seriously wounded officer, Captain Brown had immediately decided to travel to the front to render his spiritual assistance. Before the group could pinpoint the actual position of the incident they somehow managed to get lost, which in turn led them to cross into German held territory. Danger soon followed, within moments panzer grenadiers had spotted them. Once again, and so typical of Meyer, he had correctly pinpointed an area of vulnerability and had taken the appropriate steps to safeguard his lines. The untimely and one-sided confrontation quickly resulted in tragedy. The patrolling grenadiers correctly challenged the Canadians and very quickly thereafter opened fire. Whether by pure luck or by divine intervention, the short burst of gunfire left Captain Brown extremely shaken but completely unscathed! The padre's two travelling companions were far less fortunate. Corporal Greenwood was killed instantly, and Lieutenant Granger was wounded. During the ensuing panic and confusion that inevitably follows fighting, Lieutenant Granger last saw Captain Brown, about to be captured, walking towards the patrol with his arms aloft.

At this juncture, alarming as they sound, the circumstances do not amount to any serious impropriety and tend only to depict the brutality of war. However, before continuing with the narrative, two other salient points should be recognized. First, Captain Brown was unarmed and was wearing two distinctive items, a clerical collar and a Red Cross armband that should have clearly identified him as a non-combatant and entitled him to special treatment Secondly, Meyer's grenadiers should have been able to see that the approaching soldier was a padre. In spite of the time of day, (the incident occurred around 2330 hours) double summer time was in force and visibility was still fairly good. And, in addition to moonlight there were glowing embers and flames from the many adjacent fires that were still burning brightly.

When the seriously wounded Lieutenant Granger, who had been taken for dead, eventually regained consciousness, he immediately noticed that Corporal Greenwood was dead and that Captain Brown was missing. Fortunately for Granger, the grenadiers had moved on and had failed to commandeer the jeep; it had been abandoned with its ignition button intact. Miraculously, the lucky Lieutenant was able to climb aboard, stamp down hard on the ignition and drive back to the safety of his own lines.

It was a month later, around the time of Operation Windsor, (the quest to liberate Carpiquet and capture its adjoining airfield) that Captain Brown's body was eventually discovered. Surprisingly, it was found more or less in the same place where Lieutenant Granger had seen him surrender and taken prisoner. Much more startling was that a bayonet or knife wound in the chest had caused his death.

Dashboard of a Willys MB Jeep 1944.

Unfortunately, the unarmed padre's death, which bore all the hallmarks of a callous murder, was only the beginning of the many acts of brutality committed by Kurt Meyer's grenadiers. A subsequent Canadian investigation into Captain Brown's death and all the killings in and around Buron eventually revealed that twenty Canadian soldiers had been murdered and buried at the Abbaye d'Ardenne following their capture and ensuing interrogation. A total of eighteen of these murders had occurred during June 7 and 8; the final two deaths took place several days later on June 17. Later testimonies and official pathology reports (submitted as evidence during Meyer's subsequent war crimes trial) told of how the Canadian victims were positively identified by the dog tags they were still wearing at the time of death and that had not been removed thereafter. But there was far more damning evidence to come from the pathologists following the straightforward process of identification. The reports had concluded that the deaths were caused by a single bullet fired into the base of the skull, by multiple bullet wounds, or by the forceful application of a blunt instrument such as a club or rifle butt.

The thorough post-conflict inquiry instigated by Supreme Headquarters Allied Expeditionary Force (SHAEF) and senior Canadian investigators finally established that, sadly, the abbey atrocities were not merely isolated events of unlawful killings committed by a few crazed psychopaths. On the contrary, the enquiry held that during the period June 7-17, members of Meyer's "Murder Division" had unlawfully killed at least 134 Canadian prisoners of war in separate incidents.

Very significantly, the inquiry had established that the units directly involved were the 25th and 26th SS Panzergrenadier Regiments, the 12th SS Reconnaissance Battalion, and the 12th SS Engineer Battalion.[4] It also found that "where executions were by firing squads, Schmeisser machine pistols (MO-40) were usually used, and in these cases the bodies bore evidence of several fatal wounds in the torso as well as the head. In other incidents, so much damage had been done to the skull that it could only be assumed that rifle butts or clubs had been used. The question therefore, in most cases, was not whether a war crime had been committed, but what troops were responsible."[5]

In relation to command, control and overall responsibility the answer is unambiguous: on June 14, following the death of his divisional commander Brigadeführer Witt, Sturmbannführer Kurt Meyer was awarded immediate field promotion; consequently he became the youngest Brigadeführer in the German army. Meyer's promotion was almost immediately followed by a decision that would very quickly enhance the divisional makeup and fighting effectiveness of Meyer's command. General der Waffen-SS Sepp Dietrich, 1st SS Panzer Corps, reinforced Meyer's depleted Hitlerjugend with units of its parent division, the Leibstandarte SS Adolf Hitler (LAH) and an independent Werferbrigade (mortar brigade).

Having outlined the make-up of Meyer's newly acquired fighting force; the book will now focus upon profiling the mindless violence that followed. And, although committed some distance west of the Abbaye d'Ardenne, the narratives of these additional murders help provide a clear insight into the plight of unfortunate Canadians POWs!

On the morning of June 8, again only hours after D-Day, while holding a rather tenuous position near Puton-en-Bessin, the Royal Winnipeg Rifles supported by gunners of the anti-tank company and machine gunners of the Cameron Highlanders of Ottawa, were suddenly attacked by the second battalion 26th SS Panzer Regiment, under the command of SS-Standartenführer Wilhelm Mohnke. During the successful assault, approximately twenty-five to thirty Canadian prisoners were taken. After having been searched and interrogated, these dejected troops and ten others who were captured some time later were subsequently marched towards the Caen-Fontenay-le-Pesnel road and into an adjacent field. Thereafter, they were herded together before being callously shot. A number of battalion panzergrenadiers from an armoured column that had by chance arrived at the scene were held responsible. And, like many other incidents, the killings bore all the familiar hallmarks of the Hitlerjugend and their favourite weapon, the Schmeisser. The extent and nature of just what was to happen next will remain unknown, yet quite amazingly and once again either by pure luck or by a strange alchemy of spiritual intervention, at least five of the group managed to escape death by a whisker. By simply running into the high wheat fields, as quickly as their legs could carry them, they managed to avoid being scythed down and consequently made good their escape. Neither luck nor spiritual guidance was to intervene in the fate of four others that also tried to sprint to safety. Despite taking to their heels within seconds of the others they were spotted and gunned down. Although further misfortune entered the lives of the lucky five, all being recaptured, the German troops involved were far more cordial. All five were to spend the rest of the war in a prisoner-of-war-camp.

A valuable insight into Mohnke's character can be drawn by how very quickly Canadian investigators discovered (often from evidence gathered from his former troops) the full extent of the Standartenführer's ruthlessness and his apparent willingness to encourage his grenadiers to either kill in violation of the laws and usages of war or to deny any quarter.

One example that not only reveals the true extent of Mohnke's culpability but also his deplorable leadership, was the cruel murders of three Canadians who were caught in mine laying operations at Le Haut Du Bosq, on either June 7 or June 8.

Somewhat paradoxically, while busily deploying mines to safeguard Canadian positions, Riflemen A.R. Owens of the Royal Winnipeg Rifles, and two sappers J. Jonel and G.A. Benner of the Royal Canadian Engineers, were unexpectedly cut off from their units after a surprise enemy attack. Whether or not they were captured then is uncertain, but what is known, is that on June 11 all three men, surprisingly unharmed, were brought to Mohnke's H.Q. Again, after the usual insults, humiliation and interrogation; all three were marched back towards their own lines to the edge of a deep bomb crater and shot. Mohnke and several others watched over the murders.

Three days earlier, again on June 8, the Château d'Audrieu, near the tranquil village of Pavie, Headquarters of the 12th SS Reconnaissance Battalion, was to witness more brutality; the indiscriminate murder of a further twenty-six Canadian prisoners.

Away from hostilities and to some extent rather recklessly in the presence of several French civilians, young grenadiers and a few senior NCOs annoyed that earlier that day their commander (Sturmbannführer Gerhardt Bremer) had been wounded, simply lost all self-control! Amongst those callously murdered by organised firing parties, were three other members of the Royal Winnipeg Rifles, Rifleman D.S. Gold, J.D. MacIntosh and W. Thomas. Interestingly, Riflemen Gold was a stretcher-bearer and had been wearing a Red Cross armband. And, in keeping with Captain Brown, as a non-combatant should have been entitled to special treatment! Subsequently, it was discovered that these killings followed the deaths of three other Canadians who sometime earlier had been captured and had shot by their escorts. Although seemingly impossible, at about 1600 hrs that fateful day, conditions deteriorated for many more Canadian prisoners. Emulating the actions of the demonic Mohnke, several German Officers and NCOs stood by and watched thirteen more Winnipeggers being put to their deaths by way of a controlled firing squad!

As that frightful day drew to an end, and as gossip, news and morbid rumour of these and the abbey murders spread along Canadian lines like wild fire, a sunned and very angry Montgomery decided to act. Without any hesitation, he immediately appointed an investigative Special Court of Enquiry to represent British, American and Canadian forces, electing his American Assistant Chief-of-Staff, Major-General R.W. Barker as President.

Much has been made about Montgomery's prickly nature, yet regardless of the opinions of his critics or of his ardent supporters upon issues of tactics and drive, he like Churchill, very much admired his Canadian men at arms and valued their immense loyalty.

Sometime later, investigators discovered that around the same period, and within striking distance of the Château, a further seven Canadians had been killed and their bodies heartlessly left unburied. More significantly, the special investigative unit was able to satisfy the Court of Enquiry that these troops had also been murdered in the same manner as the others.

During the following day (June 9) at Bretteville I'Orgueilleuse, a crew of a disabled enemy Panzer captured rifleman L W. Lee and his colleague E N. Gilbank, of the Regina Rifle Regiment. Although both were subsequently shot, Lee, hit only in the thigh, fell to the ground and feigned death. Luckily, when it was safe to do so he finally managed to make good his escape and miraculously found his way back to his battalion. Later, grenadiers from the 12th SS Panzer Regiment were identified as being responsible for the killing of Gilbank.

On June 11, three Canadians from the 1st Hussars were taken prisoner near les Saullets. The captors were either grenadiers of the 2nd Battalion 26th Regiment or of the 3rd Company the 12th SS

Engineering Battalion. Whatever unit they originated from, they followed the Murder Divisions trademark by shooting at the prisoners after the obligatory interrogation. Quite miraculously two Canadians survived the ordeal; knowing what fate had in store, they quickly made up their minds to lie perfectly still and play dead!

Shortly after June 11, hapless villagers of les Saullets witnessed yet another cowardly shooting. On this occasion however, the same captors made sure that four 1st Hussars Canadians, would not escape.

At 1800 hrs on June 17, having been reported missing after the battle at Le Mesnil-Patry several days earlier, seven Canadian prisoners were escorted to the headquarters of the 12th SS Pioneer (Engineering) Battalion in the village of Mouen. Once again, after the customary interrogation by a bilingual senior officer, they were marched to the outskirts of the village, placed in line and executed by a firing squad. French civilians were tasked to bury the bodies.

Investigators later established that six of the Canadians were infantrymen from the Queen's Own Rifles of Canada, while the seventh was a trooper from the 1st Hussars.

Before closing this sad catalogue of brutality, there remain two other relevant issues worth noting. The first point raises the question, as to why the indiscriminate murder of Canadian prisoners suddenly came to an abrupt end after June 17, a period in which hostilities and mutual hatred were rapidly intensifying. One immediate and plausible answer might be that by then, the German forces in Normandy were now firmly on the defensive, and were convinced that the Allies were in France to stay. Meanwhile, German prisoners who had somehow managed to escape and safely return to their own lines reported that the Canadians treated them very well. Another answer might be that by then, a leaflet drop made by Allied aircraft had promised, amongst other persuasive propaganda, that those guilty of such acts would be hunted down and held responsible.

The second issue relates to the drug-addicted Nazi, SS-Standartenführer Wilhelm Mohnke. As a result of post-war investigations, not only with Canadians, but also with French civilians and many German prisoners, particularly statements made by two young Polish Hitlerjugend conscripts of the 26th SS Panzer Regiment, their ruthless leader and other less senior officers were immediately listed for apprehension and trial.

The cunning Mohnke, who was evidently disliked by his subordinates both as a man and as a soldier, was the kind of officer that was frequently described as a thoroughly evil bully and brawler.[6] Even the likes of the sybaritic Goring and the many others within Hitler's entourage, all with insufferable egos, may well have considered the former clerk as a Spiessburger (philistine) or a Piesl, (contemptuous ill-bred gentleman). Despite his obvious failings, however, Mohnke was not without courage or military guile, and in fairness to him his morphine addiction may well have been caused by his need for the painkiller following the many injuries he had sustained in Poland and France. Indeed, when fighting in Greece during the Balkan campaign, Mohnke had the misfortune to lose a foot. Despite this severe handicap, his willingness to assume responsibility was duly rewarded by the Führer, and by the spring of 1945 he had been promoted to full General in charge of a Reich Chancellery, a duty he performed exceedingly well until the final downfall of Hitler's boastful claim of a thousand year Reich.

The poignant English idiom, 'the devil looks after his own', most certainly has some merit. After serving ten years imprisonment in Russia, in itself no mean feat, Mohnke returned to Germany. He died in 2001 at the ripe old age of 91!

Four

Déjà-vu at Carpiquet

*"It is no wonder the German troops believed
Nazi propaganda about Canadian soldiers
being savages with scalping knives who
fought like wild dervishes!"*
Daily Telegraph, Special Correspondent

By July 1944, the 12th SS Panzer Division was under the command of Kurt Meyer, who had succeeded SS-Brigadeführer Fritz Witt when the latter was killed some sixteen days earlier on June 14. The increasingly bloody and vicious struggle for Caen had disintegrated into a far more bitter conflict hitherto unknown in the West. In a disastrous error of judgement Field Marshall Montgomery had faltered. Instead of hurling all available force towards the city, he had opted for more piecemeal advances that at best could only be described as cautiously optimistic. One upshot of this dogged approach was that the loyal Canadians had now been up against the ferocious Hitlerjugend for nearly a month, ever since Meyer's ambush of the 9th Brigade. Another highly significant consequence was the quite dramatic upsurge of front-line gossip. It seemed that stories of the indiscriminate murders (particularly those committed by the SS) and the ruthlessness of the gritty German resistance were not only widespread but were also beginning to take their toll on the Canadians' morale and on their increasingly fragile discipline. Equally important was the unprecedented anger and cold resentment that was rapidly gnawing its way into the ranks, and some frustrated Canadians, hell-bent only for revenge, were losing focus. Indeed, the growing acrimony towards Meyer's "zoot-suit" assassins was easily recognizable by Canadian senior officers, who were also especially aware of the strain it was placing upon their subordinates, the more junior officers and NCOs. (Meyer's troops wore loose knee-length battle smocks dotted with a mottled camouflage pattern; the Canadians quickly dubbed these excellent combat garments "zoot suits")

Contemporary accounts from several Canadian veterans familiar with and appreciative of this period clearly show the true depth of anger that they once felt. Others, have made little secret of the fact that after hearing reports of SS killings, especially of the wounded, they immediately decided that from then on the fighting would be war to the uttermost (guerre à outrance). Matters didn't end there; some veterans have intimated that even a few of their less senior officers and many NCOs had started to give guarded verbal orders suggesting that it would be easier all around if no prisoners were taken.

Unquestionably, the first few uncomfortable weeks on French soil had quickly tested Canadian resolve. German diligence and bravery had acted as a cruel reminder that the eventual capture of the city and its adjacent airfield was not going to be achieved without a savage fight. Further fuelling the highly charged situation was that for their part the Germans, especially the frequently mocking and arrogant Hitlerjugend, were well aware of the unsettling impression they had made on the enemy.

Meanwhile, the equally unfortunate British had also suffered extreme difficulties during their uncompromising June encounters. Having first languished at the hands of the Panzer Lehr Division, their situation had quickly deteriorated. Only two days after that particularly ill-fated and one-sided struggle, the 2nd SS Panzer Division had willingly joined the fray for Caen, quickly blocking any further advance southwards. Even though both the 2nd SS and the Lehr had sustained heavy losses (having been badly mauled by Allied aircraft) during their hazardous trek towards the front, the Panzer Lehr remained one of the best-equipped divisions within the Reich. (Lehr is the German word for training. With experienced instructors within its ranks, this was the demonstration division for the development of new tactics and weapons for the entire Wehrmacht, and as such was arguably it's finest and the most lavishly equipped.)

In the face of such a demoralizing dilemma, Montgomery and other senior members within SHAEF would have known instinctively that something had to be done—and done quickly—to claw back the initiative. Some historians would no doubt add that circumspect Monty was forced to think of a solution in order to protect his diminishing reputation. Whatever else may have occurred during those last few days in June, nothing could hide the fact that by the end of that month British and Canadian casualties would soon reach a staggering 25,000. This grim figure meant that from D-Day and every day thereafter, an appalling average statistic had emerged: one thousand casualties per day!

By June 30, with problems rising, especially Montgomery's recurring dream of successfully pivoting southwards and sweeping around Caen had been shattered. With the ill-fated Epsom offensive over, the need for corresponding Canadian participation was now redundant. (Operation Epsom had been Montgomery's latest attempt to capture Caen by crossing the rivers Oden and Orne - Canada's support role had been codenamed Ottawa)

Having lost the opportunity to implement Ottawa, Montgomery looked towards the Canadians for a solution. By ordering them to capture Carpiquet and its adjacent airfield, Monty first hoped to dispel any thoughts that he was failing to maintain the offensive and also rather optimistically, put an end to the increasing number of disparaging rumours of how he had lost direction.

Whatever opinion may be held on this uneasy hypothesis, the Canadian historian C.P. Stacey provides the official, rather bland account of the operation, now reclassified as code-named Windsor. "As a preliminary to attacking Caen itself, the 1st British Corps ordered the 3rd Canadian Infantry Division to capture Carpiquet village and the adjoining airfield. A plan for this purpose had been postponed on 30 June. It was revived in a more virile form - The task was difficult, the objective was held by units of the 12SS Pz-Divn, now commanded by Kurt Meyer, and the defenders were well dug in. Accordingly the plan called for powerful support."[1]

Phase 1 of the July 4 attack was to be made by the Canadian 8th Infantry Brigade (commanded by Brigadier K. G. Blackader) with the Royal Winnipeg Rifles attached from the Canadian 7th Brigade. The 10th Armoured Regiment (the Fort Garry Horse) was to provide tank support, along with special armour from the British 79th Armoured Division: a squadron each of Flails, Crocodiles, and AVREs (petards). Fire support was to be provided by bombarding ships of the Royal Navy and by twelve field, eight medium, and one heavy regiment of artillery and three companies of the Cameron Highlanders of Ottawa (M.G.) with their medium machine guns and mortars. There was a program of air attacks on pre-arranged targets, and Brigadier Blackader had two squadrons of Typhoons (fighter bombers) on call.

Apart from ordering the British 43rd (Wessex) Division to protect their right flank and to deploy a few units towards Verson and Eterville, the unlucky Canadians and seconded British units —who very much needed the Germans to believe that this was a major offensive against Caen—were in essence on their own.

After an extremely disagreeable night of almost continuous shelling and mortar fire, the order to commence operations was finally given at precisely 0500 hours. Within seconds, a creeping artillery barrage of both medium and heavy Canadian ordnance opened up on German defensive positions. Due to the diligence of Meyer's forward reconnaissance troops, his artillery units replied with a counter-barrage almost immediately and with amazing accuracy. The effects were disastrous and instantly caused considerable mayhem. As the leading Canadian troops began to move forward, they were caught by and trapped under a hail of shrapnel, As if that wasn't bad enough, as the North Shores (North Shore New Brunswick Regiment) and Chaudières advanced the bloody chaos continued unabated. Official Canadian Historian C. P. Stacey sums up the dire situation perfectly: "It caught the leading companies as they moved across the start-line, and in their advance through the level fields of ripening wheat separating them from the objectives they suffered heavily. As the men fell, their comrades marked their positions for the stretcher-bearers by bayoneted rifles stuck upright among the grain, and then pushed on."[2]

On the other hand, Meyer, who could just make out the Canadian lines amid the smoke and burning corn, would again experience the shock of combat. "We hit their assembly areas with good effect, and while the rockets howled over the airfield, I scrambled over the rubble to find Stubaf. Bernhard Krause 1st Bt. Kdr. 26 SS- Pz Regt. He had chosen a bomb dugout as his command post. From there he could observe the airfield and Carpiquet. I also saw the forward observer of Werferbrigade 7 in a bunker. A few grenadiers were about 75 to 100 metres ahead of us. Five tanks were positioned in the ruined airfield buildings. Stubaf Krause had hardly started to report on the fighting when there were crashes and shrieks all around us. The bunker shook as the 38 and 40-cm rounds from the battleships exploded nearby."[3]

Meanwhile, the Winnipeggers suffered a similar fate. "The Royal Winnipeg Rifles' attack on the southern hangers ran into trouble from the beginning, the leading companies being heavily mortared from the moment they crossed the start-line and subsequently meeting heavy machine-gun fire from the hangers themselves."[4] To make matters worse, it appears that some of the shelling from the Canadian artillery was falling short.

One of Meyer's young cadets, Schutze (Private) Kurt Misch, 12th SS Panzer Division (artillery) saw the whole sad affair from the tower of the Abbaye d'Ardenne: "The panzer grenadiers defending the airfield had the advantage of sitting in very well-built underground blockhouse, which were connected by passages."⁵ From the church spire of Fontaine-Etoupefour, south of Carpiquet, British observers from the 43rd (Wessex) Division also monitored the attack. It appears that they were terribly shaken by the rather surreal sight and the one-sided outcome: "First, the spurting, dusty smoky barrage as it crept across the green open space; next the Canadian infantry, small black dots moving steadily forward; a carefully rehearsed tattoo, the only difference being that, when the first attack failed, no drums rolled, no searchlights flashed, nor did the men lying so still get up and walk away."⁶

Further trouble quickly came the way of the unfortunate Winnipeggers; embroiled in an almost futile attack, over exposed terrain they were without close armour support. Once again, C. P. Stacey sets the scene well: "The tank squadron allotted to the Winnipeg's had been held in reserve for the first instance, and were assisting merely by fire."⁷.

Luckily, however, a greater sense of harmony was present only a few hundred metres north. All the while the hard-pressed Riflemen were clawing their way forward under a hail of intense German firepower, the Canadian attack upon the village was making slightly better headway. The North Shores and the Chaudières, despite having been shelled and mortared even before they could assemble, had somehow managed to regroup and push forward. At this point, however, it should be remembered that Meyer had reconciled himself to a temporary loss of northern hangers and village. And although he wanted the Canadian advance towards Carpiquet to be made as difficult as possible, the more infantry he could lure into the village the better. Once the victors had settled within the apparent safety of the rubble, his intention thereafter was clear: to make their newly acquired prize a living hell! To put it bluntly, he would systematically destroy the village and anyone brave or foolish enough to remain within its confines. Meyer, always the model professional, kept a record of events. "Our signals intelligence section was working superbly. Those guys had earned some praise. As a result of their monitoring we were well informed about enemy movements. This was especially true in the fighting for Carpiquet. The commander of the de la Chaudières Regiment reported the capture of the town by radio to his brigade from the centre of town. He was ordered to return but our artillery and mortar fire held him fast. Every time that he announced his departure another bombardment followed. Only about 20 of the Panzergrenadiere who had defended Carpiquet so obstinately were still fit for action. Not one single non-commissioned officer had survived. The survivors had taken over security for the 88mm battery that was positioned just to the east of Carpiquet."[8]

Among the attacking North Shores was an uneasy yet eminently proud Major J. E. Anderson. "I am sure that sometime during the attack every man felt he could not go on. Men were being killed or wounded on all sides and the advance seemed pointless as well as hopeless. I never realized until the attack on Carpiquet how far discipline, pride of unit, and, above all pride in oneself and family, can carry a man even when each step forward meant possible death."[9]

As the fighting intensified, Meyer's grenadiers quickly realized that the Canadians were in a particularly bitter mood. Sturmmann (Corporal) Karl-Heinz Wambach sums up anger:"Enemy tanks were sitting everywhere in the terrain. Three of them were on fire and, above the dug-up edge of my foxhole; I could see tanks advancing in the direction of the airfield. From a clump of trees an 88-mm fired on a hesitant enemy. This had begun about 11 am and I was still not able to free my legs and hips. Suddenly a voice yelled behind me, "SS bastard, hands up!" Two Canadians tied my hands and then hit me in the face with full force. I could hardly move my legs since I was wounded in the back, but they drove me to the rear without regard, hitting me with their rifle butts. I was tied up to a fence amidst exploding 88 shells. I must have stood there for a good three hours before they brought me further to the rear. The number of dead Canadians still strewn throughout the terrain indicated that the enemy, too, had suffered extremely high losses during the attack. Without a pause, the bitter battle continued in the distance. For me, the sad and uncertain journey into captivity began."[10]

With Carpiquet taken, Meyer's next move was to sacrifice the handful of brave grenadiers still ensnared within the village centre. Feeling truly aggrieved but refusing to be downcast, and acting in the best interest of his overall objective, he gave the order to bombard the village and bring it to its knees. The hand-to-hand fighting and carnage that followed would always be remembered by the Canadian veterans who were involved, particularly with a Chaudières captain, Michel Gauvin, who admitted that the enemy at Carpiquet had put up a most furious fight. What's more, he confirmed that unlike the North Shores, who actually bothered to take prisoners, his regiment were not nearly so obliging. In keeping with the Chaudiere's gritty motto Aere Perennius (Truer than Steel) he candidly admitted, "No one took any prisoners that day."[11] The atmosphere of mutual killing and probable hatred is to a certain degree corroborated by the Chaudières' war diary. Written accounts for the period dated July 3 to July 5 fail to record the taking of any prisoners, thus making Captain Gauvin's rather chilling admission more than just probable.

Indeed, many particularly rugged recruits within the Chaudières were called "Black Calves." A few of their forefathers had married Abenaki natives, (French-Canadian Indians, also called *bois brulé*, French for "burnt wood"). Almost all Chauds were descendants of gritty and hard-working foot-farmers who tirelessly toiled on the land, presumably with their lower leggings permanently coloured by the rich dark soil and without the aid of the vast array of modern agricultural machinery that is now so readily available. Another point of interest that became of some relevance in the struggle for Carpiquet is that although they lived a primarily agrarian life, the Abenaki (meaning "people of the dawn") were also famously good hunters and exceptional fighters. Their military heritage during the early European settlement of North America was one of unwavering loyalty to their French allies and of participation in frequent battles with those (usually native Iroquois or English redcoats) who interfered with this close-knit détente.

Although upon the outbreak of war the vast majority of Chaudières were no longer robust foot-farmers, there is no question that deep within the tightly closed ranks of the Black Calves were more than just a few extremely hard and uncompromising men. These were men who somehow simply failed to recognize the true meaning of fear and would rather risk life and limb than to be dishonoured or to experience the shame that would result from any act of spineless acquiescence or lame atonement. As the battle for Carpiquet progressed, it would be men of this particular calibre who were to clash with SS grenadiers, who in their minds were responsible for callously executing their fellow Canadians, some of whom were from another southern Quebec regiment (the Sherbrooke Fusiliers). Added to this factor is that sometimes true soldiers very willingly struggle through all the drudgery of military life for one moment of glory, knowing that just that one moment will be enough. For many Chauds, despite the strict codes and ethics that govern combat, the ensuing struggle to hold Carpiquet would provide that moment.

Meanwhile, as the North Shores and the Chauds were grimly holding on to the village, the ill-fated advance of the Royal Winnipeg Rifles was in such disarray that their commander, Lieutenant-Colonel Meldram ordered an immediate withdrawal back to the start line. Meldram had little tactical alternative; his infantry were being systematically scythed down, and his tanks were being destroyed by accurate fire from well-positioned German tanks and 88-mm guns!

Although a thoroughly dispirited Blackader had reluctantly sanctioned the Winnipeggers' return to Marcelet, matters didn't end there. In defiance of logic and determined to secure Montgomery's airfield objective, Blackader gave the order for a second attack. Even more alarming was that the second advance should begin immediately after the Winnipeg Rifles had managed to regroup and reorganize. The exceptional riflemen were equally loyal and dutiful to their task. Displaying exceptional courage, they again braved the shelling and mortar fire and pushed forward, with the forward companies repeating their earlier success by reaching the first hangars. More trouble was to follow however, the ruthless Meyer ordered his troops to intensify the shelling, and once again he even contemplated a panzer counterattack.

Amid the chaos, Meyer, in a move reminiscent of his actions at Buron, had left the relative safety of his Headquarters and had joined his grenadiers at the front. Within minutes he was brimming with admiration and pride. "The Winnipeg Rifles advanced hesitantly, not seeming to trust the empty battlefield. They moved slowly towards the first airfield building. At that point they were still about 150 metres from the hall. They had left the protective woods and were exposed on the airfield at that point. Then we heard the 'voice' we had been waiting for, 'Rat–tat-tat-tat-tat'. Our MG 42 mowed the enemy down. I jumped into a corner. The soldiers dashed out of the bunker. Not a word was spoken–they all leapt up and ran to take their old positions. Infantry fighting was the order of the day. With their sleeves rolled up and eyes directed to the front, they loaded and fired their weapons automatically. The attackers must have sustained heavy casualties. The momentum of their attack had been broken and their tanks had started to take cover."[12]

Essentially, with the Winnipeggers withdrawing for the second time, the next stage of Phase 1 (the capture the southern hangars) was aborted. Similarly, any additional action originally thought necessary for the Queen's Own Rifles Of Canada to complete the two stages of Phase 11 (capture the control buildings and preparing for a counteroffensive) would have been completely futile.

As if all this confusion was not enough, another extremely discouraging aspect that the Winnipeggers had to come to terms with was the wretched appearance of a few prisoners they had managed to capture. The shocking spectacle of seeing men first crawling, then stumbling, from huge mounds of rubble overshadowed by black smoke and grey dust was unquestionably daunting. But it made matters worse and especially galling to discover that the enemy, who had fought so gallantly and had inflicted so many casualties, were but a handful of filthy, poorly clad youngsters.

Several hours later, as natural darkness descended upon the bleak and black skies of the wretched village, and while senior Canadian officers were probably recovering from the shock of the German counterstrike that had proven to be more audacious and ruthless than anticipated, Kurt Meyer was extremely busy studying intelligence reports and reflecting on the battle's progress. Displaying every confidence in his bedraggled troops and in their characteristic determination, he true to form was planning how to re-take Carpiquet. His natural ability made him perfectly aware that the enemy were intending to make a breakthrough to the Orne bridges in Caen from the west and that Carpiquet would be an ideal starting point for fresh forces to launch their main offensive. Armed with this foresight, Meyer also quickly realized that a fresh and more daring modus operandi was needed to steal a march on the enemy. Meyer's staff officer recalls the hastily drafted plan: "The position in Carpiquet was a serious threat to the German bridgehead position. Thus, the general command ordered that the village of Carpiquet was to be recaptured and contact be established along a favourable line to the forces in action in the Odon valley. 'HJ' Division directed that 1SS Pz-Regt. (LAH) Leibstandarte SS-Adolf Hitler, (The Weidenhaupt and its second battalion came under Meyer's command) to capture Carpiquet in a night attack from the north, and defend it. Further, to establish contact on the right with Regiment 25 ('HJ') and to the positions near Verson on the left. The remnants of I. /26 ('HJ'), in action on the southern edge of the airfield, would then be pulled out. The mission to take Carpiquet in a night attack fell to III/Battalion led by Obersturmbannführer (Lieutenant-Colonel) Wilhelm Weidenhaupt."[13]

Shortly after midnight on July 5, 1944, the village of Carpiquet would embark upon hosting one of the most bitter and brutal exchanges of the entire war in the West. Of course, many historians understandably brush aside this assertion. They cynically suggest that this little-known chapter was merely a sideshow in comparison to the many-recorded incidents of brutality. Be that as it may, the level of violence at Carpiquet that summer night was as equally brutal as any close-at-hand encounter experienced by opposing infantry, no matter on what front or what particular campaign.

Fortuitously for the unsuspecting Canadians, especially the French-speaking Chaudières, and very reminiscent of the opening stages of Windsor, Meyer's night attack immediately ran into trouble. The leading company of grenadiers that had advanced towards the village was trapped by its own artillery and sustained heavy losses. After this potentially disastrous turn of events, Meyer quickly ordered a follow-up attack, and on this occasion the plan went exceedingly well. By dawn his grenadiers had reached their first objective, the railway embankments that ran along both sides of the country lane from Franqueville. Flushed with success, and despite earlier casualties from friendly fire, the attacking units continued across the railway line and raced towards the village.

As leading elements closed in upon Carpiquet village (their secondary objective), their immense courage was put to the test once more; they too were to suffer from the almost identical fate that had earlier greeted the unfortunate Winnipeggers. Meyer's grenadiers, who were busily pressing home the attack, were suddenly embroiled in a lucky Canadian counterstroke. Unlike the unfortunate Winnipeggers, however, Meyer's troops were not subjected to planned and well-coordinated machine-gun fire and mortar shells; instead they fell victim to a massive and indiscriminate artillery barrage. To Meyer's credit, with artillery hammering Canadian positions along the northern hangars of the airfield, grenadiers from his former 25th SS Panzer Regiment moving towards the French-Canadians, and the North Shore's southern flank seeking to retake the southern sector of the village; for at least a while the situation facing those front-line Canadians must have appeared extremely grim. Moreover, to many Canucks, (Canadians) especially those who had become accustomed to Meyer's boldness, those first few moments of mayhem would have unquestionably led them to believe that a full-scale German offensive had commenced.

Having been rudely awakened from their slumber, the knife carrying Black Calves were in no mood for compromise or pleasantries. Almost immediately, amid the incredible noise, smoke, and confusion permeating the atmosphere and with an amalgam of fear and intense hatred in the pit of their stomachs, several within the ranks of "the people of the dawn" realized that it was time to seek out Meyer's satanic grenadiers, wounded or otherwise, and deliver retribution. By then it seems that almost all Canadians had developed an opinion similar to Meyer's: that it was about time this particular enemy was taken out of the Caen equation once and for all!

What occurred in the dreadful melee was officially and as far as possible kept under wraps by high-ranking Canadian officers and subsequently by SHAEF. Even today there are very few books that reveal the unexpurgated story. The highly respected historian Alexander McKee wrote one such account that certainly didn't leave anything to the imagination. The unmistakable message was made perfectly clear: Canadians were just as capable of downright cruelty as the enemy, especially if they had found a way to rationalize it. In contrast to McKee's sensational account, most other historians either temper the lurid story of revenge or appear unwilling to even make mention of any callous acts of retribution wilfully committed by French-Canadians of the Chaudières.

McKee's extremely graphic version of events originates from the memoirs of Sergeant Leo Gariepy, a tank commander in the 10th Armoured Regiment (the Fort Garry Horse) who was tasked to support and protect the Chaudières during that fateful night. Gariepy is reported to have said, "You will not read it in any official document but you ask anyone who was there, and he will tell you, in a hush-hush tone. It even got into the Daily Telegraph in a backhanded sort of way, and was reprinted in The Maple Leaf Scrapbook. I witnessed a real carnage of infantry troops (Germans) in a field close to Carpiquet. The Germans had succeeded in infiltrating the advance post of the Regiment de la Chaudière, tough, rugged French Canadians who brawl on weekends for divertissement, at home. We were very close by when the alarm sounded at around 0400 hours. The Régiment de la Chaudière scurried in the semi-darkness and actually slit the throats of most soldiers they found, wounded as well as dead. This horrible carnage I actually saw from the turret of my tank at first light. These boys were actually crazed by some frenzy at being caught napping; the officers of the Regiment had to draw their pistols against their own men to make them come back to reason."[14]

Later that morning, knowing that there was little chance of success, a thoroughly disenchanted and perplexed Meyer reluctantly agreed to postpone any further attempt to re-take the village. Fully aware of the strategic importance of Carpiquet, he repeatedly asked himself the same nagging question: what more could I have done? After all, his loyal comrades from his former division (LAH) and his magnificent Hitlerjugend had again defied the odds that had been heavily stacked against them. Moreover, his grenadiers had attacked just before dawn, an extremely dangerous practice that had once more unquestionably hurt and unsettled the Canadians. Finally, how was Meyer to know that among the Canadians were those who not only considered the dawn as their special time but also would fight so ferociously? Even more telling was that on this occasion, many of his Canadian enemy would mirror hitherto SS tactics, by acting without pity and showing no quarter.

Five

THE BEAST OF CAEN

"Probably no single account of World War II aroused more widespread interest in Canada than the trial and subsequent treatment of SS, Major-General Kurt Meyer."
- Lieutenant-Colonel B. J. S. Macdonald, OBE, QC

Quiet confidence, composure, and sound judgment: Kurt Meyer, who was born on November 23, 1910, at Jarxheim, near the city of Magdeburg to the west of Berlin, possessed all these leadership skills in abundance. Yet, to well over 20,000 young protégés he frequently displayed so much more: vision, imagination, initiative, and—not least—immense courage.

While there is little need to further demonstrate these exceptional qualities, it is appropriate to highlight the decisive effect that his unique style of leadership had on the course of history. Of all the many examples of his dominant and individualistic character bursting its way into the limelight, there are two that conveniently dovetail: the fight to defend Caen and its airfield at Carpiquet and the excellent counselling of troops under his command.

However, before venturing any deeper into these topics, it is no less important to recognize that during the intense hostilities Meyer was particularly blessed with a strong supporting cast: all action subordinates, accomplished enemy commanders, and a host of wily politicians. These distinguished contemporaries also played a vital role in the month-long struggle.

But even among those who agreed with the ideals of National Socialism, Kurt Meyer's disturbingly intense infatuation with the Führer could rarely be equalled. Even more worrisome was that Meyer was in complete agreement with Hitler's views on world order under the Third Reich. Indeed, it appears that by 1944 Meyer had become the very personification of the dictatorial Nazi regime, and as such he was incapable of recognizing merit or good in any other way of life. To Meyer, only Hitler (whom he refused to criticize even after the war) could carve out a prosperous future for Germany and Europe-: a Europe free of the nefarious Jews and the evils of Communism. (A hard-nosed and devote Nazi to the core, and in total denial of Concentration Camps! In his usual calm, rather arrogant manner he conveniently suggested that he had always been well away from a bomb stricken Germany, performing military duties for the defence of the Reich. What was more damning however was his indifference and utter aloofness after he had been shown compelling evidence, not only of the existence of the camps, but also of the their truly appalling conditions. After moments of eerie silence he apparently glared at his inquisitors before calmly stating that many Allied soldiers had also acted with impropriety, especially those undisciplined gangsters who had stolen treasured keepsakes and other personnel effects from his young and very innocent grenadiers!)

SS-Brigadeführer Kurt 'Panzer' Meyer (1910 to 1961) (Nazi Party No. 316714) (Waffen-SS No. 17559)

Honours and Antecedents

Awarded the Knight's Cross: 18 May 1941 as an SS-Sturmbannführer (Major) and the commander of SS-Auflarungs-Abteilung 1. Oak Leaves to the Knight's Cross: 23 February 1943 (195th soldier of the Wehrmacht) as an SS-Obersturmbannführer (Lieutenant-Colonel).

Kurt 'Panzer' Meyer (Canadian War Museum)

Under the same command, Swords to the Oak Leaves of the Knights Cross: 27 August 1944 (91st soldier of the Wehrmacht) as an SS-Oberführer/SS-Brigadeführer (Major-General) Commander of the 12 SS Panzer Division Hitlerjugend.[1]

"The success of the 12. SS-Panzer Division Hitlerjugend was frequently due to the personnel intervention of its 34 year-old commander. His analytical skills, coupled with a sixth sense for danger and his ability to make the correct decision, enabled him to intervene personally at the right place and time. His determination and personnel example gave the soldiers - and not only from his division - the strength to persevere and to counterattack. He suffered the deaths of his soldiers as if they were his sons." - Heinrich Eberbach. General der Panzertruppen a D.[2]

To recap on events, by midday of June 14, 1944, SS-Brigadeführer Fritz Witt, commander of the 12th SS Panzer Division, the Hitlerjugend, was dead. He had been killed while personally supervising the evacuation of staff from his divisional headquarters at Venoix. Responsible for his death and the dreadful carnage that had totally destroyed the ornate French chateau were salvos from the 16-inch guns of a British battleship. As far back as D-Day, these huge naval juggernauts (HMS Rodney and HMS Roberts), sailing only a few miles off the Normandy coast and close to the designated landing beaches, had constantly rained down on a terrified—and as matters were to quickly unfold, a condemned—enemy.

The following day, on the orders SS-Obergruppenführer (General) Josef "Sepp" Dietrich and after having sought authorization from his Führer, the 33-year-old commander of the 25th SS-Regiment; 12th SS Panzer Division and fanatical Nazi Kurt Meyer was promoted, thereby becoming the youngest general within the German armed forces. Upon hearing of his appointment, the proud and jubilant Meyer turned over his much treasured 25th SS Regiment to the equally fanatical and headstrong SS-Obersturmbannführer Karl-Heinz Milius, of the regiment's 3rd Battalion. And, to reiterate upon this choice, critics of Meyer could argue that the hasty endorsement of the zealous

Milius was particularly calculating, rewarding ruthlessness above the call of duty!

In contrast, the immediate selection of Meyer to lead the division caused very few surprises, and as decisions went the choice of command was instantly and warmly welcomed. By then, not only had Meyer formed a close bond with "Sepp" Dietrich, who had always considered him to be uncommonly mature, he had unquestionably mastered all of the vital qualities of high command: energy, stamina, faith in his own abilities and in those of others, and that most important gift: knowing when and where to delegate. He was bold, innovative and original, with a mind untroubled by other people's opposing views or ideals. Added to all this was the dominance of Meyer's self-confidence, which had made him utterly fearless of death. His experiences after five years of conflict, during most of which he had been under fire, had made him intolerant of mediocrity and had strengthened his already excessive resolve. He had also acquired the tremendous mental fortitude that set him somewhat apart from other prominent leaders of that era: able to recognize both the folly of attempting to manoeuvre around the invisible and the utter impracticality of second-guessing the unpredictable. Similarly, he had developed a rather melancholy fatalism, believing that a sense of true or divine destiny would keep him from any future physical harm and secure his eventual well being. It was as though he knew that he was assured of a place in military history and that this Normandy crusade was his final chance to avenge the death of his beloved father Otto, a highly respected Oberfeldwebel (Sergeant- Major) who had died as a result of several wounds sustained in the Great War. (A protracted yet subsequently fatal disease caused by a bullet that had passed through his right lung)

To his young troops he had become a treasured and glorious inspiration. And whatever else his accusers might use as cause to berate or denounce Meyer, it would be absurd for them to contest his ability to lead and inspire in battle. A cunning innovator, he would constantly and ruthlessly challenge his opponents' tactics and their will to win. Ever since the war had started, he had acted at the centre of a blood-soaked Wagnerian stage of his own creation, performing the role as the heroic Siegfried leading his suicidal warriors to victory!

By June 1944, Meyer (an ex-shop assistant, miner, policeman, and son of a working-class factory worker) unashamedly regarded himself as an exceptional—almost gifted— upper class Prussian soldier and a commander by right. Although he had liked, respected and genuinely admired Brigadeführer Witt, within moments of becoming the new commander of the 12th SS- Hitlerjugend, Meyer began to stamp his authority on his subordinates: "Kurt Meyer began at once to reorganise the division's defences positions in preparation for the inevitable resumption of the Allied offensive".[3] For his Canadian adversaries, perhaps two of the most frightening of all his newly acquired attributes were directly linked to his Führer. The first was that despite having originated from a working-class background, Meyer was most certainly not a normal man, not even a normal soldier; he was something sui generis and a law unto himself. Secondly, by the summer of that significant year, like Hitler he was totally obsessed with the fight to save the Reich and had a clear and precise vision of just how this should be achieved. Added to these two character traits was the pleasure that the relatively young Kurt Adolf Wilhelm Meyer had begun to take in the trappings befitting a high-ranking knight in the service of his Führer.

To recap slightly, the loss of his father brought about more family responsibilities for the extremely thoughtful young Kurt, who at the age of 18 (after having graduated from the Hitler Youth) became the household's main provider by gaining employment as a miner. (An odd occupation for someone who had a phobia for the dark) After working down the pits until October of the following year, he left the mines to enrol in the Mecklenburg Landespolizel (armed provincial police). In spite of gaining promotion, his enthusiasm for National Socialism led him to join the Nazi Party and to enlist in the movement's paramilitary force, the Sturm Abteilung SA (Storm Troops). At the same time, he volunteered to serve within the Waffen-SS. Within two years, Meyer was formally accepted into the SS and was posted to a freshly raised formation, the 22nd Standarte, where he quickly gained a commission to the rank of SS-Sturmführer (2nd Lieutenant) On May 15, 1934, he was transferred into the elite Leibstandarte I. SS-Adolf Hitler (LAH), and thereafter rose rapidly in rank from SS-Obersturmführer (Lieutenant) to SS-Hauptsturmführer (Captain) to SS-Sturmbannführer (Major). In January 1942, he was promoted to SS-Obersturmbannführer Waffen-SS Panzer Corps, to which the Leibstandarte belonged.

During August 1943, after the formation of the 12th SS Panzer Division Hitlerjugend, Meyer was promoted to SS-Standartenführer and given command of the Hitlerjugend's SS-Panzergrenadierregiment 25.

Meyer initially saw combat during the conquest of Poland, and, although wounded in the shoulder during the first week of the campaign, his succeeding boldness and determination in battle quickly came to notice. His zeal and style for leading his motorcycle troops from the front earned him a second decoration, and subsequently he was awarded the Iron Cross 2nd Class to join his Wound Badge in Black.

Later in 1940, in the fighting in the Low Countries, he was awarded the Iron Cross 1st Class as well as the Infantry Assault Badge for outstanding leadership and courage. Meyer's reputation as a tenacious leader came even closer to the fore in the Balkan campaigns and thereafter in Greece, where he received the Knight's Cross to the Iron Cross for gallantry and fortitude. He was awarded Bulgarian and Romanian medals for valour. For subsequent action at Kharkov during the Russian campaign, he won the Silver Decoration for Close Combat, the German Cross in Gold, and the honour of Oak Leaves to adorn his Knight's Cross.

Operation Barbarossa made manifest Meyer's merciless determination to fight and come to grips with Germany's enemies. "Anecdotes about his method of fighting in Russia were common. He would destroy an entire village with all the inhabitants, men, women, and even small children. At another place in Russia he did the same thing in retaliation for the unintentional killing of one of his two German shepherd dogs which were said to have been given to him by Hitler."[4]

These dire claims give rise to a several points of interest. News of Meyer's outstanding gallantry during the Greek Campaign had most certainly reached his Commander-in-Chief in Berlin. And, upon hearing that the young commander was fond of dogs, Hitler had promised Meyer a puppy from his next litter of specially bred German shepherds! Of more relevance, is that during his subsequent trial for war crimes, several French personnel who had worked at the Abbaye d'Ardenne gave evidence that a large black German shepherd often accompanied Meyer. Moreover, in Meyer's autobiography Grenadiers, there are several photographs of a black German shepherd. One particular photo taken by Hubert Meyer (divisional staff officer) is captioned; 'Kurt Meyer, Fritz Witt and Max Wunsche, June 1944 in the Ardenne Abbey.'[5]

It was also at Kharkov that Meyer was given the nickname "Panzermeyer," an affectionate term of which he was immensely proud and the one that would stick with him. Incidentally, this rather macho image (thought to have originated from reckless antics during his police training) tended to overshadow his earlier nickname of "Schnellmeyer" (fast Meyer), given to him for his exploits in the Balkans. (During the course of his war, Meyer's daredevil actions, especially his insistence of leading from the front, caused him fracture over a dozen bones and suffer several bouts of concussion)

Meyer's cunning, tenacity, and outstanding leadership in Normandy earned him the right to wear the second highest German decoration for bravery in action: the Swords to the Oak Leaves of the Knight's Cross.

Before closing this short recital upon Meyer there is one particular matter that requires clarification, his experience in the handling and discipline of his troops. Without question both Meyer and his predecessor Fritz Witt, rigidly adhered to Germany's austere disciplinary system, a structure that could try and condemn to death an offender in a manner that can at best be described as indecent haste. A clear example actually occurred in June 1944, and involved a soldier in the Hitlerjugend accused of raping of a young French girl. After having been recognized as being responsible, probably by totally unlawful means when compared with today's stringent rules governing identification evidence, the defendant was unceremoniously brought before a hastily arranged court martial. Thereafter, he was then tried, convicted and executed in the space of less than three days. "Justice could be swift and punishment severe in this division where orders were disobeyed"[6] (By order of their Führer, Axis troops were authoritatively instructed to behave in a correct and cordial manner towards all French civilians, Vichy or otherwise. A directive that remained enforceable despite Normandy being under siege by Allied forces).

Six

CAPTURED AND CAGED

"I had fallen into the hands of gangsters"
(German propaganda term for both Jews and Americans)
-Kurt Meyer

Before describing the circumstances that led to Kurt Meyer's detention and trial, it is essential to briefly outline the final battles for Caen, particularly Meyer's sterling efforts to abide by his Führer's insane demand that the city should be held to the very last man! In doing so, it is also necessary to discuss Field Marshal Montgomery's constant changes of direction, especially his judgment to unceremoniously reject and jettison his hitherto overtly cautious approach to waging war, a shortcoming that abruptly came to end with his ruthless decision to bomb Caen into oblivion.

By July 7, 1944, the old Monty was gone; an increasing daring, arguably desperate leader had emerged. So striking was the change that in order to secure his long awaiting objective, a total of 2,562 tons of bombs were dropped on the Godforsaken city by a Bomber Command strike force of 467 aircraft (R.A.F Halifax and Lancaster's). Almost immediately, another more brutal episode occurred. Shortly before midnight, the city was pounded by densely concentrated artillery; 656 guns had been made available. However, this additional artillery bombardment was not the last efforts to totally crush any possible resistance from Meyer's grenadiers. Within seconds, the whining and screaming artillery shells were joined by scores of huge naval shells fired by several warships that were still lying just off the coast within striking distance of German defensive positions.

Under no illusions as to the outcome, a thoroughly dispirited Meyer had to come to terms with a far more pressing matter: the Führer's order that Caen should be defended to the last round. With problems mounting by the hour, Meyer knew only too well that to obey his leader by executing the order would definitely mean the end of his cherished division.

What was also painfully obvious was that Montgomery's broad three-divisional offensive; codenamed Charnwood, with almost unlimited recourses, was beginning to take its toll on the few remaining grenadiers in Carpiquet and other German held villages north of the Abbey d' Ardenne. Nevertheless, in spite of sustaining ever-increasing casualties, Meyer was determined to make the Canadians pay dearly for every metre of ground of the ailing Greater Reich. Amazingly, the pitiful and unobtrusive village of Buron was once again the scene of unfettered carnage. The clash between Meyer's former regiment and the Highland Light Infantry of Canada proved extremely costly with Canadian causalities mirroring those that had been suffered only a month earlier by the North Nova Scotia Highlanders.

Another worry was that way down in the bowels of the old monastery more and more of Meyer's wounded were being cared for and would soon need to be evacuated into relative safety. Determined to personally intervene and in spite of racing against the clock, Meyer quickly assembled a small battle group and hastened to their defence. By nightfall, the young Brigadeführer had once again worked wonders; although burning panzers and Sherman's surrounded the ruined Abbey buildings he had managed to bring the Canadian advance to a standstill. Minutes later, Meyer, who so often could recognize in an instant how a battle was progressing, foresaw a frightful disaster rapidly developing. He immediately began to focus all his attention on his number one priority: to evacuate the wounded as quickly as possible, taking care to leave behind only those who were seriously injured. Another essential priority would be to sensibly discard any extraneous equipment that would slow down the evacuation.

With all his dreams of victory at an end and anticipating the worst, Meyer instructed what was left of his division to commence a systematic retreat. Caen fell that night and Montgomery had finally gained the major prize of his D-Day objective. What was more upsetting for Meyer was the steady depletion of his division. Despite some success achieved by his constant and highly unpleasant counterattacks and mortar fire – particularly during August 9 when the 12th SS Panzer Division accounted for at least twenty-six tanks of the Canadian 28th Armoured Regiment, the British Columbia Regiment – his once elite Hitlerjugend was rapidly becoming a spent force. As if this was not enough, by September 4 the Division was without any serviceable tanks and lacked ammunition for the few remaining artillery units. Even more shocking was that it consisted of 600 young battle weary grenadiers.

Several days later, seizing upon a moment of surreal calm amid anguish, fear and panic, SS-Brigadeführer Kurt Meyer began to focus his thoughts on his family, especially his unborn child. Reluctantly, he decided to abandon any lingering notion of abiding by the fanatical oath that the proud and devoted Nazi had made many months earlier along with almost all of the political soldiers of the Waffen-SS. He had sworn that he would rather die than be taken alive.

I swear by god this sacred oath:
I will render unconditional obedience to Adolf Hitler,
the Führer of the Reich, supreme commander of the
armed forces, and shall at all timed be prepared as
a brave soldier to give my life for this oath.

After having managed to remove sentiment from his deeply troubled mind, Meyer shouted back to a gang of armed Belgian partisans, in particular to their leader who was with his son, "My weapon is pointing at your son. Will you keep your promise?"¹ Almost immediately the partisan replied that he would stand by his earlier promise to treat the tired and beleaguered general in accordance with international law. Luckily for the dispirited Meyer, the gang leader kept his word. Still unharmed and held in the cellar of a local church, Meyer was officially taken into custody by advancing Americans on the following day. (September 7, 1944, Liege, Belgium)

In contrast to many thousands of German soldiers who were unquestionably war-weary and more or less craving to be captured, it is perhaps worthwhile at this point to explain the gravity of Meyer's situation. As two bullish Americans charged down the cellar steps, Meyer's guard was abruptly kicked and pushed to one side, while the second American, who could speak fairly good German, shouted, "Don't resist! My buddy wants your medals as a souvenir." ² According to Meyer, after the theft of his Knight's Cross the second American, whose mother had been born in Germany, became a great deal friendlier and even displayed some compassion. Meyer was able to remember their very private, almost cordial conversation, which included this warning from the American: "For God's sake, don't tell them who you are. Your soldiers are being treated badly in the rear!" ³ The threat to his life from those who would seek vengeance must have been crystal clear to Meyer.

What really happened during this rather curious episode is yet another of the many unknowns. Although wearing the uniform of a Wehrmacht grenadier or fusilier (private) when Meyer first came to notice, if one believes his lurid account of what happened, it makes for extremely unpleasant reading. A summary depicts indiscriminate plunder, gratuitous violence, and vicious hatred: all contributing to unequivocal fear. "Before I really knew what was going on, my watch and rings were stolen. I had fallen into the hands of gangsters; (German propaganda term for both Jews and Americans) my money was stolen from me behind the Church and another GI took custody over me. Angry that there was nothing left to steal, he hit me with the butt of his weapon. After a few metres he had had enough. As we passed two frightened women, I received another blow to my back. I stumbled a few steps and returned to receive a full blow to the side of my head. As I fell I heard the protests of the women. Blood clogged my eyes and poured out of my left ear. I couldn't think any more." [4]

Whether or not the distasteful narrative is wholly accurate or amounts to imaginative fiction, the cunning Meyer, who was forever seeking excuses for the actions of his troops, made frequent references to the uncertain ordeal. This was especially so, when taxing questions were put to him during interrogation. In particular, when he was directly asked to provide an opinion upon Nazi Death Camps!

Fortunately for Meyer, most of his subsequent fourteen-month detention was spent in England, although further humiliation followed when he was unceremoniously flown back to Germany to stand trial for war crimes.

During an initial interview relating to the abbey murders, Meyer's usually well-schooled military mind was for once caught off guard, and an uncommon lack of astute self-control caused him to make several statements damaging to his own case. Intimating that he was deeply shocked by Canadian allegations he robustly rejected the accusations put to him and denied any knowledge of the callous killings that had apparently been committed by members of his former regiment. How he was to rue the day of this interview and a further interrogation that occurred on October 15, shortly before his trial was to begin! On the latter occasion, when he was asked whether or not anyone had reported to him that Allied prisoners had died at his headquarters and that it had been necessary to bury them, he foolishly replied "No" [5] The traumatic interviews had obviously increased his level of mental fatigue and had made the characteristically confident Meyer feel most unsure of himself. It appears that the courage and cunning that came naturally to him in the field of battle were curiously lacking when instead of his life, his pride and status were in imminent danger.

Suddenly sensing increasing pressure and particularly the seriousness of his dilemma, on October 26, shortly before his trial was due to begin, Meyer decided to make a fresh and more detailed statement. He had remembered that about June 10, while at his Abbey headquarters, two medical officers, the regimental doctor and the regiment dental surgeon, had visited him. The officers, he said, reported to him that there were eighteen or nineteen unburied Canadian prisoners in the garden of the Abbey grounds.[6] In a most remarkable U-turn, he explained how he ordered SS-Obersturmführer Schümann, his adjutant to investigate and as soon as the report was verified, he had made a personal inspection. After viewing the bodies, he ordered them to be buried and directed his adjutant, the legal officer, to conduct an official inquiry. No amount of speculation will ever establish the true reasoning behind this incredible volte-face on the part of such an eminent and respected soldier. Perhaps his embellished and rather patronizing account albeit highly suspect, reveals his true feelings towards the allegations, sheer indifference.

Another foolish error that the overconfident Meyer made during this unusual change of heart was to tell his investigators that he was most annoyed that his adjutant did not maintain his standard of iron discipline at his forward command headquarters. Also rather puzzling was that Meyer, who by having sacked his adjutant was obviously trying to manoeuvre himself away from accepting any overall responsibility, went on to concede that while serving in Russia, prisoners were not taken by either side! In the vain and mistaken belief that he could place blame elsewhere, he then shrewdly intimated that an unfortunate breakdown in communications had affected discipline and may have led to the revenge killings of the prisoners by a few of his men who by then had become mentally disturbed. Furthermore, he suggested that this unhappy situation was perfectly understandable because these pathetic, wretched individuals, having endured many years of constant and violent war, especially in Russia were themselves victims of cruel circumstances.

These and many other excuses were embedded in his pre-trial statement, which included an outrageous and reckless attempt, later discredited by a SHAEF enquiry, to dishonour Canadian troops. Meyer, who had earlier intimated that he had always been most cordial to Canadian prisoners, somewhat foolishly stated that before noon on June 7 (the date his regiment ambushed the Canadian 9th Brigade at Buron), while at his main headquarters at St. Germain, he had heard his men—situated well behind his forward tactical command post—talking about the killing of German prisoners by the Canadians at la Villeneuve, south of Rots. In an amazing recall of this cruel and dastardly affair, he then told the investigators that he had visited the alleged crime scene and once there, had been satisfied that bullet wounds to the head and chest had killed seven or eight of his men. He then endeavoured to somehow justify the killings at the Abbey by intimating that the unfortunate Canadian prisoners might have been killed in retaliation by a few tormented souls riled by grief and anger!

The subsequent investigation, however, quickly revealed that there were no Canadians anywhere near that that position until later that evening, thus proving Meyer's claim false. What's more, a reconstruction of that fateful morning shows that Meyer was desperately clutching at straws, attempting to not only cloud the issue of the killings but also to widen the blame and to pass responsibility to others. In an earlier admission, Meyer agreed that during the morning of June 7 he had driven to the Abbaye d'Ardenne and had taken full advantage of the splendid views that could be seen from the twin towers of his forward command and tactical headquarters. It was from this vantage point that he had waited rather anxiously for the arrival of his own regiment and as many divisional panzers as could be mustered. Given that at 1000 hours on that unforgettable morning he had taken such delight in witnessing his tanks rolling steadfastly towards him and that noon was the designated time for his regiment and units from the 21st Panzer Division to commence their synchronized attack, it is inconceivable that he could be mistaken. There is no question about Meyer's intention; he was obviously trying to cover the issue with a veil of lies.

Seven

THE TRIAL OF KURT MEYER

"The Court is not trying the German nation, nor the Nazi Party, nor the Hitler Jugend; it is trying Kurt Meyer.
- Judge Advocate, Lieutenant-Colonel Bredin

At precisely 1030 hours on December 10, 1945, Meyer, having been rushed through a gauntlet of journalists, entered the splendidly adorned temporary courtroom of the former German naval barracks in Aurich, Germany. "The Beast of Caen," as he was quickly dubbed, appeared wearing only a drab field-grey uniform without badges of rank. He stood upright in the dock and politely confirmed his name and rank in answer to the usual preliminary questions. Meyer recalled the moment: "I entered the room (a re-constructed conference room renamed Maple Leaf barracks) as a soldier and not a depressed defendant. Determined to prove myself in front of the tribunal and also demonstrate proper bearing as an example to my soldier. My judges, five generals, were sitting in front of me. I looked for and found the eyes of General Foster who had been my opponent on the battlefield in 1944. He had been designated President of the Court to pass judgement on me. What a strange encounter between two soldiers! The victor was now chosen to administer 'justice' over the vanquished after they had fought each other with every fibre of their being for months on end.

A manacled Meyer. (National Archives of Canada)

The selection of the President and his judges was impossible according to international law. All of the gentlemen had fought against me and were thus involved in the case."¹

It is not so difficult to understand Meyer's frustration. His earlier pre-war career within the police would have made him acutely aware that impartiality is a crucial element of any court hearing. Based on these circumstances, even the most narrow-minded of advocates should have at the very least argued for an independent president. Refusal to grant the legal submission would have been extremely difficult and highly improbable, and although the appointment would not have totally eliminated any counter-argument of prejudice, it would have gone some way towards displaying a degree of understanding and sensitivity. More to the point, an independent senior judge would have helped persuade the wider audience that proceedings would be fair and equitable.

Astonishingly, these proceedings were entirely lawful; they adhered to and were based upon long-established international law. Their legal foundation recognized the right of a belligerent military force in the field to try not only members of its own forces for offences against the military code but also members of enemy military forces who should fall into their hands as prisoners of war. It should also be understood that during Meyer's trial there was no official dispute over this right. Despite Meyer's deeply felt anger and resentment, the legal foundation was an agreement that both sides recognized and conveyed a power that both exercised. "Those who were critical of the machinery provided for the trial of Meyer and others should bear in mind that there was no intention to try him as if he were in an ordinary criminal court, but as a soldier charged with an offence for which he could be sentenced to death by a court martial in the field." [2]

One final point on the trial's legal foundations was that the Canadian investigators had filed evidence with the United Nations War Crimes Commission in London, summarising and detailing the offences attributed to the 25th and 26th SS-Panzergrenadiere Regiments and their respective commanders, Meyer and Mohnke. "The commission, headed by Lord Wright, a famous law Lord, and on which sat Lord Finlay, a former Lord Chancellor, and other eminent representatives of the United Nations, found that prima facie case had been established against both. Meyer at this time was Allied hands as a prisoner of war, and a wanted report was filed for Mohnke with the Central Registry of War Criminals and Security Suspects at Paris." [3]

After a short period of formalities, during which a medical certificate was produced showing Meyer fit to stand trial, the accused was told to stand, whereupon he was formally arraigned. "The first charge sheet was read to him and he, through the interpreter, pleaded 'nein' (Not Guilty) to all charges." [4]

FIRST CHARGE SHEET

FIRST CHARGE:
COMMITTING A WAR CRIME, in that he in the Kingdom of Belgium and the Republic of France during the year 1943 and prior to the 7th day of June 1944, when Commander of the 25 SS Panzer Grenadier Regiment, in violation of the laws and usages of war, incited and counselled troops under his command to deny any quarter to Allied troops.

SECOND CHARGE:
COMMITTING A WAR CRIME, in that he in the Province of Normandy and Republic of France on or about the 7th day of June 1944, as Commander of 25 SS Panzer Grenadier Regiment, was responsible for the killing of prisoners of war, in violation of the laws and usages of war, when troops under his command killed twenty-three Canadian prisoners at or near the villages of Buron and Authie.

THIRD CHARGE:
COMMITTING A WAR CRIME, in that at his Headquarters at L'Ancienne Abbey Ardenne in the Province of Normandy and Republic of France on or about the 8th day of June 1944, when Commander of 25 SS Panzer Grenadier Regiment, in violation of the laws and usages of war gave orders to troops under his command to kill seven prisoners of war, and as a result of such orders the said prisoners of war were thereupon shot and killed.

FOURTH CHARGE:
(ALTERNATIVE TO THIRD CHARGE) COMMITTING A WAR CRIME, in that he in the Province of Normandy and the Republic of France on or about the 8th day of June 1944, as Commander of the 25 SS Panzer Grenadier Regiment, in violation of the laws and usages

of war, when troops under his command killed seven Canadian prisoners of war at his Headquarters at L' Ancienne Abbaye d' Ardenne.

FIFTH CHARGE:
COMMITTING A WAR CRIME, in that he in the Province of Normandy and the Republic of France on or about the 7th day of June 1944, as Commander of the 25 SS Panzer Grenadier Regiment, was responsible for the killing of prisoners of war, in violation of the laws and usages of war, when troops under his command killed eleven Canadian prisoners of war (other than those referred to in the Third and Fourth Charges) at his Headquarters at L'Ancienne Abbaye d' Ardenne. [5]

There was a second charge sheet referring to further killings of Canadian prisoners of war at Mouen on June 17th after Meyer had become divisional commander. His responsibility here was more remote, and the convening officer authorised the prosecution to *nolle pros* this charge.[6]

Before the charges that specify the alleged violations are discussed further, the various activities that could constitute a war crime (as defined in section 441 in the Manual of Military Law) need some clarification. By its very nature, the phrase war crime tends to provoke thoughts only of acts that are totally repugnant and evil. Broadly speaking, in some respects this opinion is more or less correct; most war crimes were acts of sheer barbarism. It should be understood, however, that the term was constructed solely around a military expression and the legal sense did not include a moral dimension. Thus a war crime could relate to a covert operation requiring courage and patriotism, such as conveying information about an enemy. Brigadeführer Meyer's indictment is far less complex; Section 443 of the manual clearly covers his alleged crimes, which fall into categories; the killing of the wounded; refusal of quarter; maltreatment of dead bodies on the battlefield, and the ill treatment of prisoners of war.

A more complex and particularly intriguing issue relates to the rather woolly term, 'vicarious responsibility'. The trial would be the first occasion where the prosecution would argue that a commanding officer could be found responsible for his troop's transgressions, despite there being no direct order for doing so. Interestingly, the indirect responsibility of the highest-ranking officer on the field had been well established by The Hague and Geneva Conventions. Moreover, the conventions clearly outlined the circumstances required to establish the burden of proof. Evidence could arise from the conduct and attitude of the accused; secondly, from his failure to exercise disciplinary control, and thirdly, should the accused fail to offer any reasonable explanation. Finally, two equally important points should also be explained; Germany had been party to both conventions and Meyer had agreed to the doctrine that stated that it was forbidden to kill or wound an unarmed enemy. And, in relation to the burden of responsibility, once again Meyer was in full agreement, shrewdly adding however that if prisoners had been killed, as alleged, by his grenadiers, it was as the result of orders from someone above him in rank! [7]

CHARGE ONE:
The legal entanglements that embroil documentary evidence are endless, starting rather obviously over the question of authenticity and legitimacy. Copies, forgeries and various degrees of tampering are but a few additions, making the burden of proof extremely arduous. In the pursuit to convince the court of Meyer's guilt upon the first charge, the prosecution produced as best evidence, a copy file of secret orders issued by him during combat training in Belgium 1943, in which amongst other unpleasant commands, he instructs his troops to execute prisoners after they had been interrogated. The fourth order under the heading Behaviour At The Front was particularly relevant. It read: "The SS troops will not take any prisoners. Prisoners will be executed after interrogation. S.S. soldiers will not surrender and must commit suicide if they have no other choice. Officers have stated that the English do not take any SS soldiers prisoner."[8]

Without doubt the exhibit was at its very best highly contentious, and having read the German translation, Meyer became engulfed with rage: "When that exhibit was put on the judges' table, I did not know what to think. Was it stupidity or impudence… the presentation of that scrap of paper was an insult to the judges." [9]

In spite this forceful rebuttal during the cross-examination the prosecution decided to test Meyer's self-confidence. In an effort to regain some lost impetus, Lt –Colonel. B.J. Macdonald first told him that he considered the documentation legitimate, and went on to say that perhaps Meyer had been far too shrewd to commit such a merciless order to writing. Amazingly, the leading and particularly contradictory question produced the desired effect; Meyer unable to restrain his pride and passion began to flannel, within a mixture of innuendo and boastfulness he stated that old comrades knew how their commander fought on the basis of mutual confidence. What was even more foolish was that with typical Nazi zeal, he implied that the question had some merit! Again, only conjecture can quantify the impact Meyer's uninhibited arrogance made upon the judges. More telling perhaps was that the prosecution could now suggest that Meyer's self-righteous answer demonstrated his passive acceptance towards the line of question. Arguing that although Meyer had denied the existence of such a written order, at the very least, he had now admitted agreeing with its unrepentant ideology.

Regardless of the wilful derision exhibited by the accused, the court found both the highly damning document and the oral evidence given by at least four witnesses suitably compelling. Albeit those included several non-ethic Germans, who had been press-ganged into his former regiment, the burden and standard of proof was established. Kurt Meyer was found guilty.

CHARGES TWO AND THREE:

The court found Meyer, not guilty of the second and third charges. [10]

CHARGE FOUR:

It would be both impractical and unnecessary to examine the many witnesses who tendered sworn evidence at the trial or had earlier signed sworn affidavits which assisted the prosecution's case in relation to charge four. As matters stood, no amount of reasoned and balanced reply by Meyer's defence team could negate the shock and the initial devastating effect caused by Jesionek's meticulous and imposing evidence in chief. Despite formally rejecting several less relevant issues provided by the young pole; minor differences to his original statement due mostly to his inability to speak perfect German, the vivid detailing of how he witnessed Canadian prisoners walk calmly to their execution would have ultimately implanted an everlasting impression upon the judges, one which simply could not be ignored once heard! (Although Jesionek had agreed that his in-depth knowledge of German came only after joining the S.S., he considered himself adequately versed in the language for the purpose of conversation, an issue that had plagued Meyer's defence team from the onset).

Obviously placing great emphasis on Jesionek's early unpretentious manner, and Meyer's outburst at the abbey when he demanded to know why his troops were bothering to take prisoners, the court found little difficulty in deciding Meyer's involvement and culpability. Finally, let one issue be firmly dispensed with; the suggestion that the young Pole was harbouring a grudge against his enforced conscription. And that he deliberately sought out the war crimes commission in order to gain revenge by discrediting his former commander.

Without question, this significant theory was subjected to the most vigorous cross-examination by Meyer's defence team, yet to no avail. After several taxing questions that also suggested that the witness was seeking vengeance for his father's four-month prison sentence for refusing to use the Nazi salutation, Jesionek remained unshakable. Time and time again he denied having any personal dislike for Meyer, and insisted that he had always considered that the abbey murders were unnecessary and wrong. More importantly he had decided then and there that he would report the incident at the very first opportunity. Furthermore, although his later testimony had been delivered in a far more disagreeable manner than hitherto, his accuracy as to the terrain, weather and the conditions in the abbey was very impressive. His knowledge of officers and NCOs, including names and descriptions was equally noteworthy, and gave increasing credibility to his sordid tale. Then, just as his testimony was ending, Jesionek placed Meyer and his defence into a highly moral quandary. He calmly stated to the court that several of his colleagues had also disagreed with the earlier instruction not to take prisoners, believing that an enemy without weapons was an enemy no longer!

CHARGE FIVE:
To convict on the fifth charge the judges must have applied similar reasoning to that on the fourth charge, relying however more on the regulations. Significantly, Meyer's ill-advised and unguarded pre-trial statements added to this decision and didn't help his plea of innocence in the slightest. On the contrary, they most certainly and dramatically assisted in bringing about his eventual downfall. What's more, these subsequent disclosures—particularly the needless and terse sacking of Schümann, his adjutant—clearly implied that Meyer unreservedly accepted that it had been his troops who had committed the abbey atrocities. In the depths of utter despair, Meyer instinctively recognized that both his pride and his defence case had been severely injured by his own statements.

One final point on this issue remains totally academic: Meyer's account of the sacking was vigorously contradicted by several other of his more senior officers, all of whom spoke only of the adjutant's lack of experience. The defiant Meyer had floundered. He, not Schümann, had been the highest-ranking officer present, and as such, in charge. In plain and simple language, the buck stopped with him.

Additional Turning Points

The evidence of Trooper D-46600 Dagenais, 'A' Squadron Sherbrooke Fusilier Regiment.

Marcel J. Dagenais was a bilingual French-Canadian fusilier. His tank commander during the ambush at Buron had been Lieutenant Windsor; his crewmates had been Troopers Lockhead, Philp and Ball. Lieutenant Windsor's tank had been knocked out while assisting 'C' Squadrons efforts to repel German infantry who were fiercely attacking the depleted 'C' Company of the North Nova Scotia Highlanders. After having managed to escape the smouldering wreck, he recalls how the entire crew were captured and escorted back to the abbey, where they were interrogated by a young Sergeant Major. Dagenais' affidavit stated "Lieutenant Windsor said when questioned, that he had only three things he would tell them: his rank, name and number. With that the Sergeant-Major slapped Lieutenant Windsor across the face"[11]

Realizing that Dagenais was a French Canadian and sensing the possibility of more intensive interrogation, his captors immediately escorted him away from the others and took him to a staff car, which was then driven to Caen. Clearly, although many German intelligence officers were bilingual, after having spent four years in occupied France, most would have found the French language far more accommodating than the English spoken by their main belligerent. There is yet another possibility that should be considered; cunningly introducing his French roots into the intense but more subtle interrogation, in an effort to persuade Dagenais to believe that most of the French nation was at one with Germany and that it was the arrogant English and immoral Americans that were at fault, particularly over what they considered to be a European affair.

Whatever their reasoning, the callous striking of Lieutenant Windsor proved to be a most potent omen; for after having frustrated his interrogators, the loyal and very fortunate Dagenais, was thrown into an assembly area along with other captured Canadians. The stalwart Lieutenant Windsor was not to be seen again; his courageous stand was to cost him his life. He and the others from his group were amongst those who for their loyalty and devotion to duty had suffered the penalty of execution. In contrast, Dagenais, probably due initially to his ethnic background, survived both captivity and the war. And as a result, he had been able to provide the Court with a comprehensive account of his capture and of more importance, the appalling conduct of his captors! His highly charged affidavit concluded by announcing that whilst travelling to Caen he had witnessed Meyer's grenadiers deliberately killing wounded Canadian prisoners who had been unable to walk. [12]

The Testimony of Daniel Lachèvre.

Daniel Lachèvre, a French teenager who had lived at the abbey until mid-June was able to refute "Meyer's last minute explanation of the discovery of the Canadian bodies on or about June 11." [13] The sixteen-year-old Daniel explained how, at 8 pm on June 8, he and other boys had visited the little garden to play. Whilst there he noticed that a shelter had been constructed. He then stated that they had returned to the garden during June 9th and June 10th, yet whilst there they had not noticed any dead bodies. Most damming was that the young witness stated that the only dead bodies they had noticed was on June 14th, and they were Germans who had been killed in the recent fighting. Even more damming was that the witness Monsieur Vico; also a resident of the Abbey, who had actually constructed the swings of the play area, corroborated much of young Daniel's evidence.

Without question this contentious topic was possibly one of the most decisive turning points in the trial. It proved that Meyer had either deliberately lied or had openly disregarded the legitimacy of the allegations when they were first put to him. It also emphasised the somewhat contemptuous attitude he had foolishly displayed when he was first interrogated, denials and cloaked suggestions that coastal troops or Luftwaffe personnel had been responsible. Finally, even if by chance he had not lied over the deaths, he had been mistaken in considering that the date of any killing was irrelevant and unimportant, simply because he was not directly involved.

The Testimony of Constance Raymond Guilbert.

Of all the French civilians that testified, Monsieur Guilbert's evidence, particularly under cross-examination, was most certainly interesting. At best, he could be described as a loveable rogue with an acute sense of humour. However, before detailing his joie de vivre, Guilbert recalled the events in Authie on 7th June. He mentioned by 13.00 hrs, the Canadians had driven the Germans out of Authie yet by 17.00 hrs, different German troops returned and then drove the Canadians out. (This evidence describes accurately the Canadians' push for Carpiquet where, to recap, the Canadians cleared the villages of Buron and Authie before themselves being ambushed by Meyer's troops.) Having explained the recapture of Authie, he went on to describe how he had seen an unarmed Canadian soldier with his arms aloft and who was obviously waiting to be taken into captivity, simply shot down by advancing German infantry. He later buried the body. He also witnessed the shocking killing of an unarmed and unconscious Canadian lying under some trees in a square with German soldiers nearby. When the wounded man moved, he saw one of the Germans, an officer, take a bayonet and stab him in the body several times, killing him. Other soldiers scoffed at the body and shot into it. He also later buried this Canadian. He further stated that S.S. troops would not allow civilians to bury any bodies for several days afterwards and as they tried to pull bodies out of the road, Germans pulled them back and ordered them to be left where they were. He said that this deliberate action resulted in passing vehicles running over the bodies, with some being reduced to pulp.

Unfortunately, this extremely damning and vital evidence was somewhat tempered by the witnesses enthusiasm. Obviously wishing to convince the court that on this occasion he was telling the truth, he openly admitted that he was serving a prison sentence for looting. Rather cheekily, he said that he had discovered 2,000 bottles of wine and had brought them home and had drunk them. Thirst was the reason why he had done so. Although highly amusing, the courtroom remained amazingly subdued when his reply to the question, had all 2,000 bottles been consumed by him, was that he had lots of friends who were also thirsty!

Evidence For The Defence

Although it is unnecessary to detail all the evidence presented at the hearing by Meyer's defence team, by the time of Meyer's hearing, rumours of Canadian atrocities and counterclaims of lurid Canadian reprisals were being openly discussed within the German media. Obviously these reports and allegations were becoming the cause of uneasy concern to several high-ranking Canadian officers. As they started to enjoy the privileges that quickly follow victory, many began to ponder the actions of a number of their own troops. Meyer's unique case more than likely reminded some of them of the well-known saying "There but for the grace of God go I."

Of exceptional interest, however, is the rather eccentric evidence of Meyer's contemporaries in Normandy, General der Panzertruppen Heinrich Eberbach, commander of Panzer Group West, and his predecessor Leo Geyr von Schweppenburg. This was especially important because the rather droll general von Schweppenburg was a Catholic, a career officer (whose Prussian family had included two general field marshals) and was not particularly supportive of the Waffen SS, despite having SS Divisions under his command. Of further interest was that amazingly, General Ederbach, the only senior officer called by the defence, was allowed to present von Schweppenburg's evidence to the court, (A matter that annoyed the proud Prussian intensely, especially as he could speak English fluently and had an intricate knowledge of the British way of life and more importantly, of British military law). Why Meyer's defence team failed to call the cultured von Schweppenburg to the witness stand remains an unusual anomaly. The upshot however was not in anyway prejudicial to the bewildered defendant or his division. Not only were General Ederbach's remarks on Meyer's own abilities extremely favourable, he explained to the hearing that in full consensus with General von Schweppenburg, in terms of attitude, discipline and overall performance they had judged Meyer's division to be well above those of all other divisions that included the formidable Panzer Lehr; with a success ratio threefold to that of the 21st Panzer Division.

Ederbach's unusual evidence became even more surprising and quite bizarre when he rather shamelessly uttered a mixture of opinion, and blatant hearsay. Speaking on behalf of von Schweppenburg, yet thereafter telling the court that he agreed entirely with his counterpart's professional opinion, he did his utmost for Meyer's cause. "In my experience, a division that was not solid to its core could not continue such a performance for long. It is for that reason that I'm convinced that the atrocities were only the actions of individuals. The Canadians were brave soldiers but rough fellows. It was reported to me that they took no prisoners or shot captured German prisoners. I also had a written report with regard to that. Incidentally I read similar statements in an Allied brochure while in captivity." [14]

The Irrefutable Presumption

It is doubtful if the frustrated Meyer fully understood that in law the burden of proof can be waived where the court or hearing are able to make a presumption. A presumption is a sequence of circumstances where normally a conclusion can be drawn until, where permissible, the contrary is proved. Presumptions always fall into the following two categories. Refutable presumptions allow the court to accept that the standard of proof is beyond all reasonable doubt, unless the contrary is established. A very practical example relates to stolen property. A person in possession of stolen goods soon after the theft is the thief or handler. However, a true explanation for the possession can rebut these conclusions. Irrefutable presumptions provide the court or hearing conclusions that are rules of law in themselves and therefore cannot be disproved.

After the closing speeches Meyer, who in spite of the spirited efforts of his defence team had always suspected that a 'finding of guilt' was to be the trial's inevitable outcome, requested that he too could address the Court. After having detailed the rigorous training of his Regiment at Beverloo, he cleverly added that his men were not trained to become a band of murderers. Then in eloquently spoken German, Meyer attempted to achieve the impossible. Unruffled, yet because of constant inhibitive and interfering egotism, totally confused over the legalities that surround the terms commission or omission, or both, he somewhat waywardly decided to disprove the irrefutable presumption: that as the most senior officer in charge he was exclusively responsible for the individual actions of his troops including the hardened NCOs who had previously served upon the Russian Front. Faced with this fait accompli, and aware that he had failed in his earlier quest to implicate his adjutant, Meyer began to retract upon previously agreed decisions regarding troop discipline and officer responsibilities by shrewdly introducing to the proceedings the dehumanising effects of war. After a short period of deadly hush, Meyer, who was said to be a soldier's soldier, suddenly glared at his accusers and uttered this plausible yet altogether unconvincing and entirely invalid testimony. "I wish to state to the court here, that these deeds were not committed by the young soldier. I am convinced of it, that in the Division there were elements, who, due to the year long battles, due to five years of war, had in a certain respect become brutalised...I take every responsibility for what framework of tactical possibilities I ordered...I wish to assure the court that I gave no order to annihilate defenceless people, writing or orally...How far a commander can be held responsible for individual misdeeds of individual members of his troop the court should decide, as it consists of old soldiers... I have a clean conscience as a soldier... I wish to say I have been treated like a soldier, and the law proceedings were fairly conducted."[15]

Sentencing and Aftermath

At 1145 hrs, December 27, 1945, just twenty-five minutes after Meyer had addressed the court and had been escorted away from the hearing, the judges reassembled to give their verdict. In the breathless hush that settled over the packed room, the accused was brought before the court. The president, sternly concealing his emotion—this was for him a difficult task at a particularly poignant time of year—pronounced both judgment and sentence in a gruff voice: "Brigadeführer Kurt Meyer, the Court has found you guilty of the First, Fourth and Fifth Charges in the First Charge sheet. The sentence of the Court is that you will suffer death by being shot. The findings of Guilty and the sentence are subject to confirmation. The proceedings are now closed."[16]

With a tightened jaw, the proud Meyer bowed to the judges before being marched from the courtroom. As the drama of his departure unfolded, the resolute and unrepentant Nazi, who had learnt to live with death, stood tall, offered no other show of emotion and remained eerily silent.

Several days later, apparently persuaded to change his mind by his wife, the condemned Meyer reluctantly agreed to appeal against his sentence. Subsequently, and without seeking to challenge the courts findings or verdict he invited clemency.[17]

On January 13, 1946, Major-General Vokes, the commander of the Canadian Army of Occupation Force in Germany, who only a few days earlier, had declined Meyer's petition for leniency, commuted his sentence to life imprisonment. When subsequently pressed for a reason, he replied that he did not feel that the "degree of responsibility" established at the trial warranted the extreme penalty.[18] And, although the legal framework surrounding the decision sat comfortably within the remit of the Military code that authorises a more lenient sentence, the sudden and unexpected turn about quickly flared into a heated, national debate! Canadians at home and abroad were all asking the same question: why should Meyer escape the death penalty? Yet beyond all the rhetoric and the many thousands of genuine complaints demanding a full independent enquiry, the vast majority of those who had studied and followed the trial were very much of the opinion that the commutation of the sentence was almost certainly and significantly based on more than Meyer's degree of responsibility. Doubtless influenced by reports of various acts of revenge and retribution by Canadian troops, Major-General Vokes held the view that the death sentence passed upon Meyer was unsafe and as such was an unmistakable error of judgment. It also appears that although Vokes was an outwardly tough talking, hard-drinking womaniser and a cussing down to earth leader, he most certainly lacked both the political and military will to carry out his daunting duty. And, even before he had actually made up his mind, not only did he deliberately leak opinion that poured scorn on some of the evidence, but also quickly arranged a visit to London in order to seek both advice and guidance. Even more telling, was the fact that he sought guaranteed reassurances concerning any legal consequences that might follow an implementation of the death penalty. His hopes and cursing for good fortune to help his cause were quickly answered; during his search for an excuse to commute the sentence, a ruling that the intractable General Simonds should withdraw his keen interest in the matter certainly eased his plight. Canadian top brass then rather conveniently and perhaps outrageously sidelined Simonds, who had also fought in Normandy. They cleverly removed any possible threat he could generate by subsequently agreeing that the forthright general was the senior Canadian officer in the Netherlands, a different theatre than Normandy. Having made this point, the official version of events state that the resolutely outspoken Simonds wanted nothing to do with the trial!

It is only conjecture, yet it appears that General Simonds, who during the beginning of August 1944 had brought a fresh and daring tactic to Normandy by attacking the enemy at night, was more of a military hawk than the outwardly rough-necked, yet politically minded Vokes, and as such, was far more in favour of the death penalty. Indeed, it is well known that Montgomery, who had decided from the outset that Meyer's trial was solely a Canadian affair, had great admiration for Simonds even though he had been labelled as rather a loose cannon requiring firm handling. On the other hand, the straight-laced Montgomery had very little respect for the openly barefaced Vokes. Despite all his terms of endearment for the ordinary soldier, Monty could be scathingly critical of his fellow officers; and it appears that the prickly Field Marshal neither admired nor approved of Vokes, whether as a spirited soldier or as an astute commander. Unfortunately, this character assassination did not stand alone; several of Vokes's junior commanders had earlier put into question his decision-making. One described Vokes as being likeable enough but an infantryman, pure and simple, and an infantryman who hadn't a clue on how to operate an armoured division, while another, Lieutenant-Colonel Proctor, who felt so strongly about the loss of two companies from the Lincoln and Welland Regiment, went to Corps HQ and requested a transfer. He had disapproved of his commander's ill-fated decision to use war canoes as transport, which resulted in the drowning of many men as the canoes were holed and sunk by enemy fire. Proctor was subsequently granted his request and promoted.

With controversy over Meyer, gathering pace at break neck speed, Lieutenant-Colonel Macdonald, Chief Prosecutor during the trial was utterly distraught. Rejecting the opinions of those who held a contrary view, particularly those who were quoting the biblical idiom about casting the first stone, his mindset was much more in tune with the feelings of others. This was especially so, with those that questioned why high-ranking officers appear immune from any responsibility? The articulate Macdonald, who had actually fought against Meyer and knew only too well the fanaticism of his troops, not only expressed his disappointment to his superiors but remembered the public's ensuing outcry: "My personal reactions to the decision of General Vokes were as nothing apparently compared to the surge of anger from Canadians everywhere at home. Thousands of letters, telegrams and resolutions of protest descended on Ottawa.

Municipal councils, Canadian Legion posts, the press, and every kind of organisation as well as thousands of citizens everywhere, went on record as opposing the commutation. So great was the volume of replies necessary that twelve form letters were devised to answer adequately the various objections raised."[19]

On September 7, 1954, ten years from the day that American Forces had captured him, Meyer, the Beast of Caen, was released from custody. In the midst of the storm surging round him (which was fuelled by a vilifying Canadian media), Meyer maintained a dignified calm. His unquestionable loyalty to the SS never faltered, nor did his continued drive to actively defend his membership and that of his former comrades. Paradoxically, Meyer began to shoulder the burden and blame while simultaneously protesting his innocence, as if no one were culpable This proud and intense crusade (especially his battle to have war pensions awarded to former members of the Waffen-SS) persisted until December 23, 1961, when on his fifty-first birthday he died of a heart attack. His wife, four daughters, and a son survived him.[20]

Meyer's funeral was attended by a gathering estimated at 5000 mourners; many were ex-members of the Waffen-SS who had travelled to Hagen from all over Europe. A tribute to his exceptional military career was included in the eulogy. Meyer's former staff officer Hubert Meyer ended with these words: "Wherever we are, privately, publicly, at home or abroad we will say with pride: 'I...was a comrade of Panzermeyer'! In that way, you'll always be with us, your influence will continue on! We salute you Kurt!"[21]

Eight

MURDER IN WAR IS STILL MURDER!

"The hero was not Kurt Meyer."
- Lieut-Colonel B. J. S. Macdonald O.B.E Q.C.

In concluding this short yet highly dramatic commentary on the military career of Brigadeführer Kurt Meyer, there remain two outstanding questions. First, was Meyer really guilty of war crimes? Secondly, could Meyer have prevented Hitlerjugend atrocities, particularly at the Abbaye d'Ardenne?

Predictably, the answers to these highly charged questions entail many difficult variables, not least, because of the huge diversity of opinion that war whatever its justification tends to generate. Another factor that needs consideration, particularly in this rapidly changing world, is the relentless drive to spread political correctness into almost every aspect of daily life, let alone every individual action taken by those engaged in waging vicious combat. As if this is not enough, with the aid of video telephones and other highly sophisticated technology, war has become yet another form of reality TV. An instant media commodity, that can cross examine and discuss complex rules of engagement in the relative safety of a debating studio many thousand miles from the actual war zone. And, of more relevance, constantly scrutinise the conduct of those at the front and in the very thick of the fighting!

Although care should be taken not to entirely discount these more contemporary views and rather sanitised attitudes, this analysis commences by utterly rejecting one beguiling explanation given by Meyer after his most fortunate yet inappropriate release from custody. During his relatively short period of freedom, Meyer suggested that it had been virtually impossible for him to admit to an enemy court that such things had been done and that therefore it had been far easier for him to lie about the executions and to find excuses for his gallant and innocent comrades.[1] On one other occasion, he skilfully elaborated on this spurious rationale. Without any regard for the feelings of those who were still mourning the loss of their loved ones, he rather manipulatively implied that as soon as he had identified the NCO who had killed at least seven of the eighteen Canadian prisoners at the abbey, he had promptly ordered the culprit to stand guard at a completely untenable forward outpost. Not surprisingly, Meyer continued the story by proudly boasting that the war-weary, homicidal member of his non-commissioned staff was killed almost immediately at his new post.

Also firmly suspect are several pious words Meyer wrote in his outstanding autobiography Grenadiers. In this very worthy testimonial, initially to his much favoured regiment and thereafter to his treasured division, Meyer expressed a great deal of satisfaction in his clear memory of the ambush of the Canadians, which had occurred within shelling distance of his abbey headquarters. Then he explained how, immediately thereafter, dedicated teams of German medical personnel had tended to wounded grenadiers and to several injured Canadians. As previously cited, he clearly recollected, "The doctors and medics didn't look at the uniforms. There was nothing to separate them at this point. The only thing that mattered was saving lives." [2]

While there is little doubt that these statements were true and that many of his young grenadiers and several of his NCOs displayed a common soldier's mercy to badly injured troops, this is not the legitimate issue under review and as such has little bearing. What is relevant is that the wounded no longer presented a real and continued security threat to his forward command post, and, of more importance, they didn't interfere with Meyer's ability to utilize all of his effective fighting force. No small part of the problem presented by non-injured prisoners was that commencing with their capture there was a necessity to deploy guards, devise duty rosters, and provide prisoner escorts when the time arose. However, the wounded, after having received basic first aid, could have been dispatched immediately to the relative safety of the rear echelons. Once there, they could receive further medical treatment and be interrogated if at all possible. Although this would have been an obvious drain on his resources, Meyer would have known that the tiresome responsibility would require only a few ancillary personnel and one or two medics. However, since every trained grenadier was invaluable to his plans, the fit and able prisoners were considered an impediment to the fulfilment of Meyer's obligations. Much more troublesome was the knowledge that these captured troops presented a more realistic threat, despite the fact that they were unarmed and herded together like cattle. Meyer also knew that regardless of their particular plight, if so minded they could try to assess and evaluate his resources, especially his regiment's strength in numbers, transport, and weaponry. Furthermore, regardless of rank, each and every one of them could convey such useful information to the enemy if by chance an escape route presented itself in the rapidly developing fog of war. Perhaps the astute and ruthless Meyer was considering these possibilities at the abbey, especially at the moment when he carelessly and rather angrily pointed out to those around him that unlike the seriously wounded, these prisoners would all require German provisions or rations for sustenance.

It is also appropriate to reflect upon Meyer's rather animated reputation. Like many other notorious individuals, his deeds—in his case on the battlefield—were seldom seen with any sense of true proportion. Reports of his exploits, regardless of their level of accuracy or verifiability, more often than not attracted either extravagant praise or ardent condemnation. Clearly, then, there is a need to ignore some of the flamboyant rhetoric, whether adulatory or censorious, before a balanced judgment can be reached.

Finally, the old adage that there are no bad soldiers, only bad officers, can also be wholly dismissed. This is so in spite of Meyer's immense pride continuingly bursting towards the forefront of his trial, where during his cross-examination he had foolish agreed with this worthless comment. Indeed, the cliché is puerile nonsense and tends to cloud the issue of actual blame. Furthermore, it also negates any soldier's individual responsibility for his own actions. One can only reflect upon the sheer delight of the prosecution team after Meyer had somewhat arrogantly shouldered the blame for his men actions. The proverb 'pride goes before a fall' seems quite apt! On a parallel theme is the equally invalid excuse "I was only following orders," as this, too, attempts to cloak an individual's personal accountability.

With these issues in mind and regardless of how much this interesting topic is debated in future, it must also be remembered that Meyer's case serves well as a reminder of what can happen during the bloody intensity of war. Indeed, to those caught up in the violence, war provides the full spectrum of human emotions and of behaviour ranging from exceptional deeds of heroism to acts of extraordinary evil. Somewhere in between lie other potent feelings: hopelessness, pain, despair, and the loss of dignity. All these additional depressing emotions and circumstances make for truly desperate times. Similarly, during unyielding conflict and periods of bitter revenge, desperate people very often commit acts of cruelty without having any regard for the future. To them, the future—either immediate or distant—seems irrelevant. Added to this are survival instincts that are deeply imbedded in our genetic makeup, thus enabling even the most timid of personalities to behave completely out of character. Occasionally, this almost involuntary overreaction can frequently lead to the use of gratuitous violence that hitherto would never had been considered.

After many moments of indecision and much reflection, the conclusion remains unchanged and unaffected: Meyer was guilty as accused and as indicted. Not only was he guilty of committing war crimes in Normandy, there is evidence that he had also previously contravened the codes and ethics of waging war in Belgium, where he endeavoured to incite troops under his command to discount the taking of prisoners. A re-examination of the many and varied accounts of how Meyer conducted his private war before and during June 1944 shows that he unquestionably allowed "war to the uttermost" to tarnish his splendid military record. In particular, his barbaric actions in Russia speak for themselves.

More than this, his conviction was justified in light of the evidence submitted at his trial, which was fairly conducted under the terms of military law. Although it was at odds with the views of many other commanders who were unable to prevent individual soldiers from seeking revenge or committing acts of downright cruelty and therefore to some degree empathized with Meyer, this issue should not have mattered, nor should it have prevented his lawful execution.

Two further critical factors arise: Meyer's irrepressible character and his actual whereabouts at the time of the killings. There can be little argument about the audacious Meyer's ability to influence and manage his young troops. He was such a truly inspirational leader of men—with a resolute code of conduct and discipline aided in its purpose by an almost mystical charm—that it is inconceivable that any of his grenadiers would purposely fail to comply with any but the most minor of his regimental orders. This is especially so in respect of the treatment of prisoners. In war, as in life, other incidents of petty theft and physical or mental abuse were commonplace; although repugnant, they were still a very far cry from premeditated and callous murder. It has to be accepted that the individual actions of a few insane or heartless soldiers in the heat of battle offer a serious understanding of war, although never an excuse. However, the cold-blooded killing of uninvited prisoners by utterly ruthless troops manning a forward regimental command post is quite another matter.

This point intensifies when the second and rather more controversial issue is examined: Meyer's whereabouts during the progress of those cruel killings and his ability if so desired, to intervene. Here again, hindsight and misrepresentation have played their parts, with Meyer deliberately stating that at the time of the abbey killings he was at his main Regimental Headquarters at St. Germain on the outskirts of Caen. The earlier inquest refutes this spurious claim and reveals that Meyer, who was revered by his young troops and his more senior NCOs, was known to be only a few footsteps away from their adopted killing ground. What's more, he was most certainly close enough to actually hear the first and subsequent loud pistol shots that took the lives of those helpless Canadian prisoners. After having heard the first shot echo around the sacred grounds of the abbey, Meyer again displayed sheer indifference. At a result of his inaction, the issue of who abetted, counselled or procured the order to shoot or indeed who actually committed the killing immediately became academic. By doing nothing to prevent the additional deaths, Meyer callously embroiled himself in further acts of inhumanity. For a principled officer of such high standing, his conduct was utterly unforgivable. What's more, this opinion can sit comfortably within a sound and tested legal framework. "Under British and Canadian law no distinction is made as to guilt between the one who actually commits the offence and him who is only party to it." [3]

Before closing this judgement upon Kurt Meyer's responsibilities, guilt and seemingly revered reputation, endeavour to place aside his outstanding bravery especially under fire. Equally irrelevant and therefore should also be disregarded, is his incredible ability to effectively and lawfully wage war. Having done so, focus and reflect upon the shabby and unworthy excuses put forward by Meyer when questioned about the evil of Nazi concentration camps; that allied soldiers had had stolen watches, rings and other keepsakes from his own troops. Undeniably, Meyer's amazingly terse responds was not lost on someone in the know, and by far the best qualified to pass judgment: his old adversary both on the battlefield and in the courtroom, Lieutenant-Colonel Bruce J. S. Macdonald, OBE, QC. "His state of mind is well illustrated by this astonishing comparison, which he solemnly offered as an excuse for the bestialities performed by the men wearing the same uniform as himself."[4] Finally, reflect upon the poignant last chapter in Macdonald's accomplished publication The Trial of Kurt Meyer that reads as follows: "Who, if anyone, emerges as a hero from these proceedings? It was the Canadian soldiers (those who were executed at the Abbaye d'Ardenne). They died bravely as prisoners of war in the best traditions of the service, because they would not betray their comrades or their country by giving information to the enemy. The hero was not Kurt Meyer".

POSTSCRIPT

"Meyer is typical of the kind of German it would be most dangerous to let loose in Germany once again" [1]
- Milton Shulman (Canadian Intelligence officer)

Whereas the appalling encoding of Germany's youth during Hitler's reign of terror has been acknowledged and discussed, there arises another significant observation; after Meyer gained his freedom, what was life like for the devout Nazi known as the Beast or Butcher of Caen?

Taking care not to duplicate previous accounts of Kurt Meyer's highly dramatic military dexterity, in response to this decidedly probative question, the following short postscript may well prove to be enlightening. As a result, there will be those who will probably believe that the fearless and dashing commander truly deserved his long awaited liberty. On the other hand, there will most certainly be others that consider Meyer's much acclaimed later years that were comparatively free from additional recrimination or punishment, as an unpalatable insult to justice. A point of view that becomes more significant when due consideration is extended to the families of those innocent Canadians, who were so cruelly executed.

Whereas opinions may well differ, there can be little doubt over Meyer's sudden and quite dramatic change of fortune. After an extraordinary even-handed trial and thereafter a lucky escape from death by firing squad, Meyer was hastily transported to far away Canada. Once embarking upon true Canadian sovereignty and whilst under intense secrecy, the fortunate Meyer was immediately dispatched to Dorchester Penitentiary in New Brunswick. Although very typical and now fully expected of our modern day press, especially its aggressive almost intrusive journalism, the news of Meyer's rather secretive move to Canada was still nevertheless quickly established. As a result, all the major newspapers and legislative journals covered the story of his unwelcome arrival in immeasurable depth. Almost immediately, further revelations were soon to hit the headlines. In spite of being lodged with common criminals, the Beast of Caen was hastily granted the privileged position of trustee and was assigned to work in the much cherished prison library. Whilst there, not only did he learn to speak English, but by all accounts he quickly made an extremely favourable impression with all those he came across, from fellow inmates to the prison chaplain.

Whatever input Meyer's own persona may have generated, the controversy that followed his trial continued unabated and within months of his incarceration, a growing number of supporters petitioned to have his trial reviewed. These newfound friends that also included several prominent German born Canadians all believed that he had been unjustly convicted. Having started a pressure group they pinned their hopes and lobbied vigorously on the grounds that the prosecution evidence had been wanting, vague and unsafe. In spite of the petition failing, the outcome left most Canadians with uneasy feelings of mistrust and complete dissatisfaction of the whole uncomfortable affair. None more so, than those who were utterly convinced of Meyer's guilt and had hoped and expected the death penalty. And, in striking contrast, those who had always considered the trial unwarranted and had been a dreadful miscarriage of justice!

Of greater significance was Meyer's post-trial reactions and demeanour. According to C. W. H. Luther, (Ph. D. in Modern European History) who has written several articles specifically on German military history, despite increasing challenges and unsettling setbacks, Meyer's intense loathing of Soviet Russia never faltered; this was so, in spite of his faithful driver and close confidant Michel, being a much admired Cossack. Always utterly convinced that the Soviet Empire would constantly find the time and the reason to do whatever it liked, and when it liked, he prepared pages of unsolicited tactical recommendations for the Canadian Army based on his own dramatic experiences gained at the Eastern Front. Meyer's unquestionable talent and insider knowledge of Russian paranoia, especially of the West was speedily recognised. Subsequently, within only a matter of weeks endless processions of military personnel from the National Defence Headquarters, Ottawa, were ushered into the secret bowels of the penitentiary to warily study improvised maps and diagrams, while listening intently to Meyer's numerous theories. Even more alarming was that in acceptance of Meyer's tactical acumen, the Canadian top brass eventually utilised his skills, briefly appointing him as an official military advisor. And amazingly, went as far as to allow him to wear a Canadian Officers uniform! Despite Meyer's willingness to contribute, the veil of secrecy that masked his advantaged position, helps foretell the anger that the bizarre, albeit temporary assignment would have generated, especially with those many thousands who disagreed with the unexpected commutation of his sentence.

Any beneficial outcome that may have resulted, and quite why this highly unorthodox arrangement came to an abrupt end, remains another unknown. Yet, according to Dr Luther, in October 1951, the Canadian government quite suddenly transferred Meyer to the British prison for war criminals at Werl, West Germany, some ten miles from Dortmund. Evidently luck or more likely, favourable connections continued to play a part. Although officially held in solitary confinement, Meyer somehow managed to meet and socialise with other convicted German leaders, including Feldmarcshall Kesselring, a favourite of post war veterans affiliated with several neo-Nazi organisations.

By the summer of the following year however, all was not well for the hitherto fortunate Meyer, many years of hardship and battle weariness had began to take its toll, and his health was rapidly deteriorating. Suffering from an amalgam of arthritis, defective kidneys and high blood pressure Meyer was eventually hospitalised with ailments culminating in a tonsillectomy (complete or partial removal of the tonsils) that nearly proved fatal; shortly afterwards he suffered a mild heart murmur.

In June 1953, another bizarre twist entered the unpredictable life of Kurt Meyer; he received a particularly controversial visit from the West German Chancellor, Dr Konrad Adenauer. In a highly charged meeting, not only did the Chancellor publicly shake the former SS general's hand, but also promised to do all he could to end his imprisonment! Without doubt having friends in high places prevails: during the early morning of September 7, 1954, exactly ten years to the day that American forces had officially taken Meyer into Custody he was released.

Whether or not Meyer's freedom was politically engineered also remains conjecture; nevertheless his release most certainly placed the Western Powers into an uneasy quandary. Meyer was still wanted for war crime atrocities in Russia, a theatre of war where upon his own admission; his conduct appears to have both sardonic and cruel. True to character however, Meyer's outpouring of scorn and contempt for the Red Army, was tempered by an insistence that his troops were only mirroring the actions of the barbarians that they were up against! (As an aside, during Meyer's interrogation, the distressing news of dire Soviet revenge and retribution upon both German soldiers and civilians alike would have been common knowledge). Notwithstanding this factor, his excuse for shooting prisoners was equally unrepentant. Without displaying any feeling of remorse whether genuine or otherwise, Meyer had explained that on the occasions he had fought in Russia, his unit had always conducted offensive operations, and that all had been carried out well behind enemy lines. It was these mitigating circumstances that had made it impossible for him to offer safe conduct for the captured. Although by then pointless and purely academic, it appears that the question of how Meyer treated the Russian wounded was never mentioned apart from once incidence when he rambled on about survival of the fittest. Expanding upon this unpleasant topic, there is little doubt that as a result of successful Nazi propaganda, regardless of their country of origin or rank, most troops serving in Hitler's SS-legions, especially the brainwashed Hitler Youth were highly politically and racially motivated. It is also worth stressing that based upon a regime purposely designed to introduce an ideological hate-war against wicked Jewish Bolshevism, devout Nazis and many less bigoted military personnel considered Bolshevik Russian's and those born within its host of authoritarian satellite states, Untermenschen - racially inferior!

With Meyer's immense hatred for Mother Russia, and the recently expanded eastern block (forerunner of the Warsaw Pact), it is easy to fully appreciate the sensitivity that surrounded his release. And the tense aftermath that would have occurred if by chance he had fallen into the hands of a new enemy, communist Germans who had quickly adopted to a fresh totalitarian regime and had become steadfastly, almost slavishly loyal to their new Soviet masters!

So typical of the industrious Meyer, despite much uncertainly as to his future, he immediately embarked upon two far more wholesome projects. First, he took up employment as a sales coordinator for a local brewery, with the additional responsibility of supervising 27 sales representatives. His success was such that within a few months he was managing to sell Andreas bottled beer to the messes of Canadian armed forces serving throughout the free Europe! In contrast, although his second mission was inwardly guided by a political agenda, the overriding cause was outwardly humanitarian - seeking justice for his Waffen SS comrades.

Ignoring union leaders that were predominately of the left and politicians of the right and centre right, the only administration Meyer openly supported was the Hilfsgemeinschaft auf Gegenseitigkeit des Angehorigen der chemaligen Waffen-SS, a veteran's organisation that gave financial and emotional support to former members of the Waffen SS. Within three years of his release, again as previously stated, Meyer who had become of HIAG's principle spokesmen was busily haranguing the Bonn government to provide SS veterans equal pension entitlements to those comrades that served in the German Wehrmacht. Whereas all his many appeals and lectures were equally rousing, probably the most absorbing was made in Karlburg in July 1957, where Meyer's true character came to the fore. The proud and passionate orator unashamedly delivered a litany of stirring analogies, many of which were highly charged in political innuendo:

A human being will not survive these troubled times without some sort of compass, which at least gives him the general direction in which to proceed, That's why we first have to re-establish absolute values and enter binding obligations.

We, that is, everyone who believes they can still help their nation and humanity in these times…not because it appears to offer success from the outset but, instead, because it is the right thing to do.

We that is, all those who have not dedicated their lives to the satisfaction of material goods but, instead, have dedicated it to a meaningful cause…. My comrades, we must participate in this work if we are more than just a club. The intellectual breakthrough will happen one day, and we must not stand around like camp followers…. We must build fortresses within our families, within our professional environment, the circle of our comrades. These fortresses of morality, of strength of character and of decency!

After forty months of intense campaigning and with a little more than a degree of irony, 1961 became a pivotal year for the increasing fatigued Meyer. Influenced by the trial of the notorious Nazi henchman, Adolf Eichmann who had been captured by Israeli agents, then hung for his key role in the holocaust, the Bundastag government expressed extreme caution. With SS atrocities once more making uncomfortable headlines, Meyer's efforts to have the Waffen-SS deemed a military force identical to the Wehrmacht fell upon deaf ears. What was agreed upon however was a fudged compromise; inasmuch, as means tested financial support would be granted to veterans afflicted by genuine hardship. As ever, the tenacious and uncompromising Meyer fought on. (Ironically, several years later, when the German administration finally succumbed to Meyer's well-intended wishes, more drama unfolded. As a result of Meyer's posthumous success, the once wanted war criminal Wilhelm Mohnke became a legitimate claimant!)

During the evening of December 23, 1961, less than six months after having suffered this highly political set back, and after telling his daughter Gerhild that he felt unwell, Kurt Panzer Meyer, suddenly and unexpectedly died of a heart attack. Although he had earlier suffered two mild strokes, his larger than life approach had managed to convince almost everyone that he was as invincible, (defiant to the end, he had refused to give up his liking of rich food and cognac).

Without question, his untimely death was a complete and unwelcome surprise. Not only were his family, close friends and companions stunned by the sudden news that was to quickly spread around Western Germany but also, an escalating number of devoted followers, particularly amongst his former Waffen SS colleagues. These included many who had managed to escape from the Soviet regime that had since engulfed the East.

The injustice of unexpected loss together with a genuine outpouring of grief spoke volumes for Meyer's mounting political influence. Indeed, such was the intensity; it could now be argued, that the short period of freedom Meyer had welcomed and enjoyed, had very quickly witnessed the dawn of a new leader apparently by divine right. However, what was more pertinent and somewhat chilling was that despite deliberately manoeuvring the Waffen SS ex-servicemen organisation away from any political movement, and explicitly breaking any former ties with several neo-Nazi groups, beneath a veneer of moderate pro-Western righteousness, a young, dynamic, and ardent anti-Bolshevik Führer was unwittingly being created by stealth!

To rebut those that may suggest that this possibility is simply exaggerated folly, and that Milton Shulman, the Canadian Intelligence officer was wrong in his written assessment of Meyer; several other caveats should be remembered. First and foremost, before 1945, over six million people belonged to the official Nazi Party, with several million others being involved with affiliated organisations. And, although these figures obviously suggest a potent power base from which to re-ignite the Nazi political will and its inexcusable excesses, the figures also reveal the Volk available to refill the mystical vision of a Germanic Heimat or homeland and empire (Reich) - an unusual 'collective psychoses phenomena', which was still firmly embedded within early post-war German society. (Volksgeist / Germanic soul). A fixation fuelled by mass hysteria that first arose during a period when Germany was spit into thirty-three states, and where ethnic Germans formed part of communities in almost all of its neighbouring countries: Russia, Poland, along the Baltic, through Czechoslovakia and Hungary, Romania and as far as Croatia. A point not lost on Hitler and his minister of propaganda, the sinister yet brilliant orator, Joseph Geobbels during their earlier quest for power. And, enshrined by the poet who encouraged the Germanic peoples to support the Crusades, Walther von der Volgelweide (*c.* 1170-1230) - Ich habe lande vil gesehen so – I have seen many lands!

However, without wishing to stray from any discussion upon Meyer's military and social attributes, apart from his acute hatred for Jewry and Soviet hordes, it is also worth considering the other main Nazi doctrines that he believed sacrosanct and that held the key to developing European and world order; eugenics and euthanasia devised to breed racial purity by any means possible; the creation of a Teutonic master race by way of prohibiting union between Aryan and non- Aryan peoples. And finally, as previously discussed the war against Untermenschen, by way of expulsion and mass murder!

With these disturbing factors in mind, it should also be remembered that Allied public and political attention was increasingly being distracted by the onset of the Cold War, and the retreat from European Imperialism both in Asia and in the Indian sub-continent.

Another point, which is of equal importance and which tends to moderate this rather emotive topic, is that only a very small fraction of the 1,000,000 members of the Waffen SS served within the evil Special Action/Task Groups (Einsatzgruppen) or were directly involved in any reported war crime. What's more, it should also be understood that the majority of these dedicated soldiers, very often acted with the utmost dignity as well as exceptional courage. Indeed, with a degree of irony, there are several sources that depict incidents of uncommon compassion by the 12th SS Panzer Division. (A truly astonishing example was at le Mesnil-Patry, when Meyer's young troops permitted Canadian ambulances and Red-Cross personnel collect the fallen and wounded).

Finally, in spite of the many catastrophic setbacks to their political and social objectives, what motives for a better life remained embedded in their mindset? Whatever else might have influenced them, history shows that most German veterans, Wehrmacht and Waffen SS alike, and many of their offspring retained an intense hatred of Stalin and his Soviet Ivans. Especially reviled, was Russian post war policy that ordered German prisoners-of-war to be detained in special camps, or Spetslager, sometimes set in former nazi concentration camps. Also without question was that regardless of their SS-Reichsführer's (Heinrich Himmler) principal role in the "Final Solution", as a response to the presence of Jews and other demonised minorities, the vast majority also remained doggedly loyal to the few more oblique and humanitarian aims of National Socialism: respect and devotion to family, community, country and head of state. (Perhaps many still yearned for a wholesome, idyllic Europe, rich in children bred by holders of the Mothers' Cross set in bronze, silver and gold, a Europe that was free of swindling racketeers, charlatans, and more importantly void of worthless, work-shy scroungers that the devious and despotic Führer had promised). This extreme patriotism was particularly recognisable in a staggering 99 percent of officers and non-commissioned officers of the establishment. Officers and NCOs who remained defiant, despite having been incarcerated in Allied prison camps for up to four years, and having been forced to attend German de-Naziification courts. Officers and NCOs who refused to display any remorse for taking firm action against reprobates and criminals. And, for waging war against a soviet regime riddled with evil communalist and promoters of anonymous mediocrity. Perhaps more chilling was that very few claimed to be burdened by any personal guilt.

To recap, on 28 December 1961, at Hagen, Westphalia, Kurt Meyer was finally laid to rest. (The cemetery is now known as the Eduard Muller Krematorium.) Controversial to the end, Meyer's funeral was the largest that Hagen had experienced. Several thousands condolences were also received and as a result extra postal staff were drafted in to deal with the huge number of telephone calls, telegrams and letters. Even more telling was that along with close family and friends; several eminent politicians together with many thousands of Waffen-SS comrades from all over Europe attended the packed congregation. And, from all accounts, it seems that many more thousands of dedicated admirers and would be followers, lamented the cruel loss to the fatherland!

History tells us that with the passing of time, old wounds and prejudices tend to heal and fade. There is evidence that the German people are not exempt from that general rule. On a humid, Sunday morning, July 6, 2008, Meyer's grave and headstone looked rather worse for wear. The neat engraving that depicts his name and the Iron Cross are now rather difficult to distinguish, and although the grave is still tidy, there is little evidence that suggest that the deceased was once part of the so-called glorious Third Reich.

As an aside, not one local florist (there are florist adjacent to most cemeteries in Hagen), or taxi driver had knowledge of Meyer. Furthermore the clerk at the railway station's information desk appeared most alarmed at my plea for assistance, and when finally satisfied that he was not addressing a neo-Nazi, stated that he could not help. After almost three hours and by way of diligent police enquires, via their military police colleagues, Meyer's grave was finally located. (The seven cemeteries and additional small burial grounds in and around the district had presented difficulties) This outstanding piece of public relations was provided by two young and extremely modern looking patrol officers, both of whom appeared captivated and utterly astonished by the thought of someone travelling from England to visit the burial place of a convicted Nazi war criminal. Indeed, both officers emphatically stated in perfectly spoken English what they thought of Germany's Nazi past, 'a shameful era of terror and almost unbelievable inhumanity – a period of history that continues to be taught at college as part of the National curriculum'!

Kurt Meyer's Grave.

PHOTO CREDITS

Dedication	Abbaye D'Ardenne: Commemorative Plaque *Author's Collection*
Page 22	Abbaye d'Ardenne *Author's Collection*
Page 27	Meyer's 'Zoot-suit' Hitlerjugend *The Imperial War Museum*
Page 36	Dashboard of a Willys MB Jeep 1944 *Author's Collection*
Page 59	Kurt "Panzer" Meyer *Canadian War Museum*
Page 74	A manacled Meyer *Nation Archives of Canada (PA 132444)*
Page 109	Kurt Meyer's Grave *Author's Collection*

BIBLIOGRAPHY

Copp, Terry and Bechthold, Michael. ***The Canadian Battlefields in Normandy, A Visitor's Guide***. Waterloo: Laurier Centre for Military Strategic and Disarmament Studies, 2004.

Foster, Tony. ***Meeting of Generals***. London: Methuen Publications, 1986.

Luther, Craig W.H. ***Blood and Honor: The History of the 12th SS Panzer Division***. San Jose, James Bender Publishing, 1988.

Macdonald, Lt Col. ***The Trial of Kurt Meyer.*** Toronto: Clarke, Irwin & Company Ltd, 1954.

Masure, A, ***Abbaye d'Ardenne, June 1944.*** Buron, Calvados France: L' Association des Amis du Canada, 1984.

McKee, Alexander, ***Caen: Anvil of Victory.*** Souvenir Press, 1964.

Meyer, H. ***History of the 12. SS-Panzerdivision Hitlerjugend***. Winnipeg: JJ Fedorowicz Publishing, 1994.

Meyer, Kurt. ***Grenadiers.*** Winnipeg: J.J. Fedorowicz Publishing, 2001.

Rohmer, Major-General. ***Generally Speaking***. Toronto: The Dundurn Group, 2004

Stacey, C P. ***Official History of the Canadian Army. The Victory Campaign***. Ottawa 1960.

Zuehlke M. ***Holding Juno.*** Vancouver/Toronto/Berkeley: Douglas & McIntyre, 2005

ENDNOTES

Introduction
1. Rohmer Richard. Generally Speaking. p. 105

Chapter I. Push for Caen.
1. Stacey C.P. Official History of the Canadian Army 'The Victory Campaign.' p. 126
2. Meyer H. The History of the 12 SS Panzer Division "Hitlerjugend". p. 41
3. Ibid. p. 41
4. War Records Sherbrooke Fusilier Regiment.
5. Stacey C.P. Official History of the Canadian Army 'The Victory Campaign.' p. 128
6. War Records Sherbrooke Fusilier Regiment.

Chapter II. Ambushed.
1. Macdonald Lt-Col. The Trial of Kurt Meyer. p. 5
2. Meyer K. Grenadiers. p. 226
3. Ibid. p. 226
4. Foster T. Meeting of Generals. p. 311
5. Luther Dr. Blood & Honor. The History of the 12 SS Panzer Division. p. 143
6. Ibid. p. 144
7. Study of General-Major Feuchtinger loc. Cit p. 25.
8. Meyer K. Grenadiers. p. 229
9. Zuehlke M. Holding Juno. p.124.

Chapter III. They Only Eat Our Rations.
1. Luther Dr. Blood & Honor. The History of the 12 SS Panzer Division. p. 181
2. Macdonald Lt-Col. The Trial of Kurt Meyer. p. 110
3. Ibid. p. 110
4. Luther Dr. Blood & Honor. The History of the 12 SS Panzer Division. p. 183
5. Macdonald Lt-Col. The Trial of Kurt Meyer. p. 33
6. Ibid. p. 190

Chapter IV. Déjà vu at Carpiquet.
1. Stacey C.P. Official History of the Canadian Army 'The Victory Campaign.' p. 153
2. Ibid. p. 154
3. Meyer K. Grenadiers. p. 256 & 257
4. Stacey C.P. Official History of the Canadian Army 'The Victory Campaign.' p. 154
5. McKee A. Caen: Anvil of Victory. p. 195
6. Ibid. p. 195
7. Stacey C.P. Official History of the Canadian Army 'The Victory Campaign.' p. 154
8. Meyer K. Grenadiers. p. 258
9. Copp T. & Bechtold M. The Canadian Battlefields in Normandy. A Visitors Guide. p. 57
10. Meyer H. The History of the 12 SS Panzer Division "Hitlerjugend". p. 136
11. Foster T. Meeting of Generals. p. 333
12. Meyer K. Grenadiers. p. 257 & 258
13. Meyer H. The History of the 12 SS Panzer Division "Hitlerjugend". p. 139
14. Foster T. Meeting of Generals. p. 334

Chapter V. The Beast Of Caen.
1. Meyer K. Grenadiers. p. 406
2. Ibid. p. 2
3. Luther Dr. Blood & Honor. The History of the 12 SS Panzer Division. p. 207
4. Macdonald Lt-Col. The Trial of Kurt Meyer. p. 75
5. Meyer K. Grenadiers. p. 325
6. Macdonald Lt-Col. The Trial of Kurt Meyer. p. 40& 41

Chapter VI. Captured And Caged!
1. Foster T. Meeting of Generals. p. 401
2. Meyer K. Grenadiers. p. 306
3. Ibid. p.306
4. Ibid. p.306
5. Luther Dr. Blood & Honor. The History of the 12 SS Panzer Division. p. 189
6. Ibid. p. 189

Chapter VII. The Trial of Kurt Meyer.
1. Meyer K. Grenadiers. p. 354
2. Macdonald Lt-Col. The Trial of Kurt Meyer. p. 39
3. Ibid. p. 37
4. Ibid. p. 89
5. Ibid. p. 90
6. Ibid. p. 90
7. Ibid. p. 44
8. Meyer K. Grenadiers. p. 355
9. Ibid. p. 354
10. Macdonald Lt-Col. The Trial of Kurt Meyer. p. 187
11. Ibid. p.124
12. Ibid. p. 124
13. Ibid. p.152,153
14. Meyer K. Grenadiers. p. 363
15. Macdonald. Lt-Col. The Trial of Kurt Meyer. p. 193

16. Ibid. p. 194
17. Ibid. p. 196
18. Ibid. p. 199
19. Macdonald. Lt-Col. The Trial of Kurt Meyer. p. 200
20. Luther Dr. Blood & Honor. The History of the 12 SS Panzer Division. p. 194
21. Meyer K. Grenadiers. p. 406

Chapter VIII. Murder in War is still Murder!
1. Masure A. Abbaye d' Ardenne June 1944. p. 16
2. Meyer K. Grenadiers. p. 229
3. Macdonald. Lt-Col. The Trial of Kurt Meyer. p. 209
4. Ibid. p. 79

Postscript.
1. Macdonald Lt-Col. The Trial of Kurt Meyer. p. 206

ACKNOWLEDGEMENTS

A word or two of thanks

I am extremely grateful to all those who have encouraged me to continue writing about the Canadians in Normandy. Indeed, several have taken the time to either write or e-mail their congratulations. A few have explained how the outstanding courage of the extremely loyal Canadians during the intense and bloody campaign for Normandy was in many respects, hitherto unknown. Equally, a fair number were quite stunned by the appalling indoctrination of Germany's youth during Hitler's reign of terror, while others, were utterly astonished by the fighting qualities of the Hitlerjugend.

Special thanks however must be given to the following: To Ben Kooter, President of Vanwell Publishing Limited, St Catherine's, Ontario, Canada. For almost six years, he has shown faith in my writing abilities and his professional advice has been appreciated. To my close friend, Owen Miles who together with Graeme Wadhams designed the front cover making my vision come true. To reiterate, special thanks to Mark Warner, Director of Kall Kwik who together with David Bedford, his technical wizard, made the book possible.

Finally I need give my belated thanks to my beloved father, *"Ti-pit"* (colloquial Québécois for little-boy) Leonidas Jean Joseph Gilbert (Trooper D 46221), a French-Canadian tank gunner, who served with the Sherbrooke Fusilier Regiment, Royal Canadian Armoured Corps. During the years we spent together, although in no way ultra patriotic and with a typical lack of flamboyance, he would occasionally and rather modestly bless me with several poignant anecdotes about his war in Normandy. By the time of his death, Moi et père nous sommes un! We were as one. I will always remember his unconditioned love.